the
5 Sex Needs
of
Men and Women

DR. GARY & BARBARA ROSBERG
with Ginger Kolbaba

TYNDALE HOUSE PUBLISHERS, INC.
CAROL STREAM, ILLINOIS

Visit Tyndale's exciting Web site at www.tyndale.com

TYNDALE and Tyndale's quill logo are registered trademarks of Tyndale House Publishers, Inc.

The Five Sex Needs of Men and Women

Designed by Ron Kaufmann

Edited by Lynn Vanderzalm

The names and some of the details in the illustrations used in this book have been changed to protect the privacy of the people who shared their stories.

Library of Congress Cataloging-in-Publication Data

Rosberg, Gary, date.
  The 5 sex needs of men and women / Gary and Barbara Rosberg with Ginger Kolbaba.
    p. cm.
  Includes bibliographical references.
  ISBN-13: 978-1-4143-0183-9 (hc : alk. paper)
  ISBN-10: 1-4143-0183-9 (hc : alk. paper)
  ISBN-13: 978-1-4143-0184-6 (sc : alk. paper)
  ISBN-10: 1-4143-0184-7 (sc : alk. paper)
  1. Sex—Religious aspects—Christianity. I. Rosberg, Barbara. II. Kolbaba, Ginger. III. Title. IV. Title: Five sex needs of men and women.
  BT708.R62 2006
  248.8'44—dc22   2006009725

Printed in the United States of America

12 11 10 09 08 07 06
7   6   5   4   3   2   1

To

Jerry and Nancy Foster

Mike and Linda Colby

Tim and Michelle Vermillion

༄

It has been a joy to walk as four couples through life in friendship and accountability since 1979.

We have been with each other as our children have been born, as they have been raised up in Jesus, as many of them have been married, and as we are now in the grandparenting years.

We have celebrated memories together and even grieved the loss of parents together.

Let's now finish strong together in our marriages, friendships, and impact for Jesus Christ!

We love you all.

༄

CONTENTS

ACKNOWLEDGMENTS

"You are writing what?" We can't tell you the number of times we heard that question when we mentioned we were writing a book titled *The Five Sex Needs of Men and Women*. We heard curious questions and saw some red faces. But most people said, "I can't wait to get my copy."

Why the strong responses to this book and title? We believe it's because God created sex and has a great plan for your marriage in the area of sexual intimacy. But there is also another reason. We believe that many, if not most, Christian couples have been so overwhelmed with messages about sex that they are confused, concerned, and have truly legitimate questions about what a great sex life in a great Christian marriage looks like. The book you are holding has been labored over like all of the books we have written, but this one has a unique capacity to really give you, a husband and wife, a great deal of insight, coaching, and inspiration to have the best sex life you could ever imagine. And like all of our books, this one has been a team effort.

At the core of this team have been three women who have used their gifts, talents, and time to minister to us—as well as to you. The first person we want to acknowledge is Ginger Kolbaba. Ginger is the managing editor of *Marriage Partnership* magazine. She is well respected in the field of marriage literature, and when we identified early on that we wanted a strong collaborator in the writing, her name was at the top of the list. For several days, tucked away in a historic river city along the Mississippi, Ginger met with us and helped craft this message. She brought her skill, humor, and passion for marriage to every page. Thank you, Ginger. Truly, without you this book never would have been written.

Second, we commend Sarah Carroll for a job well done. Today Sarah is a stay-at-home mom with her new baby daughter, but for several years she worked alongside us as our radio researcher. We first met her when she was fourteen years old and submitted an essay for a radio contest on our program. She won the contest hands down. She then interned with us as a college student, eventually holding a vital role as our researcher for our daily radio program. Early on in the development of the manuscript for this book, she labored with us, crafting the early stages. At the end of the project she jumped back into the game and helped immeasurably by tracking down footnotes, sources, and more. Kudos to you, Sarah! Your talent is outmatched only by your passion for your marriage and for being a mom.

And third, we want to thank Lynn Vanderzalm, our editor. Lynn was one of the first people we met years ago at Tyndale House Publishers. And from the first meeting to the editing of our first Tyndale book, *The Five Love Needs of Men and Women,* and then on to eleven other book projects, she has been our champion, helping to forge out the best books we had in us. We heard Lynn referred to as the "velvet hammer" by another writer, and it describes her well. With love and grace she works with authors to keep digging down deep to bring the best message to readers. More important, she is a dear friend, and we honor her with this book.

We also thank our team at our ministry, America's Family Coaches, as well as our board of directors, who equip us daily to do what we are passionate about doing: speaking and writing in different ways—from radio to books to conferences—so we can speak into the hearts of marriages in America and beyond. Everyone who comes into contact with our team and board comments that they are remarkable folks. And they are that—and more. We love you and thank you.

Thanks to our other friends at Tyndale: Ron Beers, Ken Petersen, Carol Traver, MaryLynn Layman, and more. You make us look far better than we are, and we thank you for your partnership but much more for your friendship. It is a great experience doing books the old-fashioned way, through a relationship. We promise to honor Jesus with this book.

And finally, we thank our kids and grandkids, who once again sacrificed time with Papa and Gaga Rosberg (that's us) so that we could write a book. We promised you we wouldn't embarrass you with this topic of sex, and we don't believe we did. What a joy to be your mom and dad and grandparents. Our legacy is rich with passion for marriage and Jesus Christ. It doesn't get any better than this, kids. Now guard your hearts, and go back to doing what you do best . . . loving Jesus, each other, and us!

Gary and Barb Rosberg

CHAPTER 1

It's Not Just about Technique

When we were preparing to write this book, we took a weekend and drove six hours to a small tourist town where we would be free from distractions and interruptions. On our last day there, as we were walking to a restaurant for lunch, our daughter Sarah called us on our cell phone. She sounded panicked about what we were writing.

"Mom," she said, "you're not writing a technique book, are you?"

"Why? Would that be a problem?"

"Are you going to talk about your sex life?"

"Yes, Sarah, we're telling *everything* about our sex life." Barb laughed as she imagined the panic in our daughter's eyes. "Absolutely, lots of detail. No holds barred. Will all your friends want a copy?"

As it turned out, Sarah's phone call was prompted by a conversation she'd had with five of her friends—all of the women are married twentysomethings. "During our quilting time," Sarah said, "we were doing our usual thing, talking and laughing, when one of the women steered the conversation toward sex. She said, 'I bought one of those technique books, because I want to please my husband—and experience some pleasure myself!'

"Well, everyone started shrieking and laughing, and then they all admitted that they had bought technique books too.

"Mom, you know I don't usually talk about stuff like this, but I mentioned that you and Dad were writing a sex book. Everybody's eyes got really big, and one of my friends gasped and said, 'Your *parents? Ewww!* Will there be illustrations? They're not going to talk about their own sex life, are they?'

"I said, 'I certainly hope not,' but then I realized I don't know *what* you are going to write about.

"One of my other friends thought it was kind of cool. She said, 'How many parents are willing to be that open about their sex lives?' But then somebody else said, 'Yes, but would *you* want to read the details of *your* parents' doing it? I mean, the mental pictures alone would be enough to put me in therapy for years! It's just . . . *ewww.*'

"So, Mom," Sarah said nervously, "I really hope you and Dad aren't going to embarrass me."

As we ate our lunch, Barb recounted the conversation with Sarah. "I find it fascinating that these young women have all purchased books about sexual techniques. When we were first married, we never would have thought about buying that kind of book. But can you imagine if we had? I would have been so embarrassed. But now Sarah's generation is not only buying sex technique books—they're proud of it."

"I think it's great that Sarah and her friends want to make their sex lives as fulfilling as they possibly can," Gary said.

"There are certainly some good books out there about sexual technique, but I'm a little concerned that by focusing on technique and the physical aspects of sex, they may miss out on the deeper, more fulfilling aspects of a great marriage relationship. Marriage is so much more than sex, and sex is so much more than physical pleasure and technique."

Certainly there is a place for learning techniques—and practicing them—in our sex lives. When we get married, it's not as if God opens our brains and pours in all the wisdom we will need for sexual satisfaction. But it doesn't take long to realize that great sex involves more than just physical intercourse. A mutually satisfying sexual relationship—the kind that grows and matures and flourishes over the full life of a marriage—has more to do with bonding, emotional connection, mutual submission, and putting the other person's interests above your own than it does with positions, pleasure points, and physical technique. Intercourse is a *part* but not the *whole* of sex.

Great sex involves more than just physical intercourse.

THE MYSTERY OF SEX

One of the reasons we decided to write this book is that sex has the potential to be the most profoundly satisfying and rich part of a marriage. Sex the way God intended it to be expressed— within the context of a loving, serving relationship between a husband and wife—is a mysterious and sacred act that knits a couple together in ways that are beyond description. We can talk about the deep, toe-tingling pleasure of orgasm, but words fail when we try to describe the oneness that a husband and wife feel after giving their bodies to each other. The Bible tells us that this oneness is a reflection, a mirror, of the oneness between Christ and his body, the church: "'A man leaves his father and mother and is joined to his wife, and the two are united into one.' This is a great mystery, but it is an illustration of the way Christ and the church are one."[1]

Sex the way God intended it to be expressed is a mysterious and sacred act that knits a couple together in ways that are beyond description.

Although sex can lead a couple into some of the most intense pleasure in a marriage, sex also has the potential to lead them into pain. Why is that true? First, the very mystery that we just described can lead to misunderstanding between husbands and wives. When we conducted a survey for our book *The Five Love Needs of Men and Women*, we learned that *intimacy* was the number two need expressed by both husbands and wives. However, we learned that men spell *intimacy* s-e-x and women spell *intimacy* t-a-l-k. (We'll discuss these differences in later chapters.) Second, most of us come to our marriages with unrealistic expectations about sex, expectations built on media images of sculpted bodies and steamy seductions. We measure our own experiences against what we see on our television and movie screens or what we read about in books, and we feel disappointed. Maybe even cheated. Third, our sexual lives can cause hurt because we too often see sexual pleasure as something we get rather than something we give; we are more focused on our own needs than on our spouses'. A great sex life leaves no room for selfishness.

A great sex life leaves no room for selfishness.

Deeply satisfying sex occurs when husbands and wives connect the physical with the spiritual, emotional, relational, and psychological sides of sex. When all these facets work together, couples enter the mystery of the oneness God intended.

God created men and women to be sexual beings. Yet very few topics are as confusing as the role of sex in a marriage. When we teach about sex at conferences, the atmosphere in the room changes. Some people can't wait to hear us talk openly about a topic that's often not discussed. Others are curious, almost as if they're trying to figure out what is normal. Still others can't believe we are going to talk about sex in a mixed audience; for them, the topic is taboo, something Christians do not discuss—certainly not in public and more than likely not in the privacy of their relationships either. Many couples experience guilt, shame, or confusion. Some feel resigned to the idea that sex will never be what they expected or desired.

If we took seriously the glimpses that movies, television programs, and books give us into people's bedrooms, we would conclude that singles or people in extramarital affairs have the best sex. Well, they don't. Medical studies have discovered that married people have the best, most satisfying sex. They enjoy sex more often and have the highest levels of physical and emotional fulfillment. In fact, 88 percent of married people receive great physical pleasure from their sexual relationships, and 85 percent report the same positive experience emotionally.[2]

The gold standard of research on sex in America is a 1994 national survey conducted by a team of University of Chicago researchers who interviewed 3,400 people. When the researchers asked respondents how sex makes them feel, married people outscored single people in every measure of delight. "Not only are married people the most emotionally fulfilled—telling researchers they feel loved, wanted, and taken care of while in each other's arms—but they also report high levels of physical pleasure. Far from considering monogamy monotonous, 91 percent of husbands and wives say they aren't just satisfied with their sex lives, they're 'thrilled.'"[3]

Sex is extremely, intensely satisfying—when it's used the way the Creator designed it. That's when it works best, when it lasts longest, when it brings strength to a relationship, and when it elicits ecstatic responses from husbands and wives.

Would it surprise you to know that some of the most erotic writing about sex is in the Bible? The book called the Song of Songs records King Solomon's conversation with his beloved, and he spares no detail in describing his intimate love for her. God loves great sex. And if he's placed his stamp of approval on it in the context of marriage, then that must mean it's something worth doing—and pursuing.

Great sex isn't just a grope, a grab, and a romp in the sack— although at times it can be. Great sex involves a lifetime of study and practice. It requires commitment and discipline.

Great sex isn't just a grope, a grab, and a romp in the sack—

although at times it can be.

DISAPPOINTMENT ABOUT SEX

Even with all of the statistics about how great married couples do in the bedroom, in Gary's work as a counselor and in our work coaching people through our ministry America's Family Coaches, hosting our national radio program, and speaking at national conferences, we've seen literally thousands of people who have problems with sexual intimacy. In many households, couples are confused and disillusioned about sex.

When we meet with people, we hear lots of disappointment and dissatisfaction. We keep asking ourselves why married Christians are struggling so much with sexual intimacy. Of all people in the world, they should have the best, most incredible sex lives. After all, they worship and serve the great creator and designer of sex! But it is clear to us that Christian couples are struggling just as much as, if not more than, their non-Christian counterparts.

A few years ago we surveyed hundreds of couples from across the country to find out their top sex needs, their desires, and their struggles. The majority of this book is based on our findings in that survey.

There's one thing we want to be clear about right up front. When we discuss sexual needs throughout this book, we do not necessarily define them the way many other authors of sex books do. Many books discuss specific techniques or other options relating to what takes place during intercourse. We define sexual needs as what goes on both *inside* and *outside* of the bedroom. What is or is not going on outside the bedroom has a profound impact on what goes on inside the bedroom.

What is or is not going on outside the bedroom has a profound impact on what goes on inside the bedroom.

In a sense, this book is a story of how you can make sure you and your spouse have the kind of sexual intimacy you've always longed for. And the good news is that it's never too late.

If you are dealing with a sexual issue in your marriage—no matter what it is—we want you to find the hope, encouragement, and healing to pursue great sex. If you and your spouse are not experiencing a satisfying sex life, then we want to set you free from what is holding you back, lead you to an open discussion, and ignite a desire to seek God's best in your bedroom.

Our hope is that this book will be a winner's manual for you. We want you and your spouse to have a winning relationship. If you're going to run a race, you don't want just to say you ran a race—you want the trophy!

Before you read any further, think about your sexual relationship. How would you rate yourself as a couple? Are you generally satisfied but want to kick it up a notch? Are you disappointed, left wanting a deeper sex life? Are you in serious trouble?

In chapters 3 through 7 we will discuss the top five sex needs expressed by the men and women we surveyed. But before we do that, write down your responses to these four questions:

1. What are your top five sex needs?
2. What would your spouse say are your top five sex needs?
3. What do you think are your spouse's top five sex needs?
4. What would your spouse say are his or her top five sex needs?

Each of these questions is important. Not only is it important for you to understand your own needs—how can you communicate your needs if you don't know what they are?—but you need to understand your spouse's needs too. Not just what you *think* his or her needs are, but what they *really are*. Most of us live with a Golden-Rule mentality in our sex lives: If I treat my spouse the way I want to be treated, then we'll be happy and have a fulfilling sex life. But as you have probably discovered and as we'll discuss often in this book, men and women are different, and they have differing sex needs. Only when we understand these unique needs—our own and our spouses'—will we be able to have deeply satisfying sexual relationships in our marriages.

Most of us live with a Golden-Rule mentality in our sex lives:
If I treat my spouse the way I want to be treated, then we'll be
happy and have a fulfilling sex life.

As you can see, this exercise will take some careful thought and some open communication. Some of you will be ready for that; others of you won't. When you talk to each other, be respectful. Sex needs are not easy to discuss. Listen with the goal of understanding, not judging. Ask clarifying questions.

It's all right if you are not completely aware of what your sex needs are. Reading this book will help you deepen your understanding. Your statement of your needs may change as you read the book and try various things. That's okay too.

When you read the results of our survey, you may agree with the majority of the respondents—or not. The point isn't whether or not you match up with the survey; the point is to help you grow in your awareness of your spouse's needs and of how you can meet them. You or your spouse may have needs that don't even appear in our list of top five needs. Does that mean you are weird? Probably not. Each of us is unique, a one-of-a-kind creation of a loving and wise God. *Understanding* your spouse's uniqueness and committing yourself to *meeting* those unique needs should be the goal of a satisfying sexual relationship.

Understanding your spouse's uniqueness and committing yourself to *meeting* those unique needs should be the goal of a satisfying sexual relationship.

So, if your needs are different from those listed in the survey results, do you need to read the book? We think you should, because the underlying principles apply to a variety of needs. Even if your needs are not quite the same, read through each of the chapters. We know you will learn things that will challenge you to make different choices, to ask probing questions, to take steps toward becoming sexually one with your spouse.

Each story we share is based on real couples' experiences, although we've changed names and some aspects of their stories to protect their privacy. We hope their stories will assure you that you are not alone in the issues you and your spouse face.

Many times we may talk in generalities and break down issues by gender. We want to make clear, however, that although these differences are found in a majority of people, they are not by any means the defining experience. Sometimes these differences are reversed: Maybe, for instance, the man is more in tune with his emotions and the woman is more focused on the physical side of sex. If this is where you find yourself, please know that that is okay. You and your spouse are not abnormal if you don't necessarily fit within our research statistics.

Although we will highlight sex needs and issues, we don't want to leave you without practical help on how to move toward deeper sexual intimacy. Each chapter includes lists and suggestions to get you started right away. Don't allow the lists to overwhelm you. Pick a few actions that make sense for your situation, and concentrate on those. Even though we can give no absolute guarantees or quick fixes (anything worthwhile requires effort and attention), we do believe our suggestions will set you firmly on the path to a stronger and more fulfilling sex life.

Throughout this book we may say or suggest things that offend you. Rather than throw the book across the room, first stop and really think about what we're saying. Ask God to shed light on those things that may cause you grief or anxiety or anger. Ask yourself why those statements bother you. Is it because there may be a kernel of truth that you haven't been willing to face? We hope you will be open and willing to accept some things that may be difficult to take but that may bring a positive, lasting change to your sex life—and to your marriage.

CHAPTER 2

Redefining Sex

In an episode of the long-running television sitcom *Home Improvement*, Tim "the Tool Man" Taylor and his wife, Jill, have a conversation about her best friend, who is dating Dave, a friend of Tim's. One day Dave tells Tim that he is seeing another woman on the side. When Jill learns this from Tim, she immediately starts to call her friend to tell her the truth. Tim objects, "Look, Jill, it's none of our business."

When Jill tells Tim that he needs to have a talk with Dave, Tim objects again: "Men do not call each other and talk about relationships."

"You talk about *sex*," Jill says.

"Sex is not about relationships," Tim shoots back. Then after a raised-eyebrow look from Jill, he adds, "Except in ours."

To which Jill replies, "Until now."

Tim represents a common perspective in our culture: that sex is its own entity, separate from relationship. We see this over and over in our society. Sex is perceived as the ultimate goal. There's a focus on "doing it" and "hooking up," with no expectation of a commitment between the two people. Even within marriage sex can become something we worship, an idol of sorts.

Although sex within marriage is definitely important, it is not the only part of marriage that is worth pursuing. Sex is simply part of the whole fabric of marriage. We can never experience truly satisfying and fulfilling sex apart from relationship. In other words, we can't have one without the other. Although many people try, the results are inevitably devastating.

We can never experience truly satisfying and fulfilling
sex apart from relationship.

God created us to be relational. Increasingly our culture disconnects sex from relationship. But sex is part of relationship. That's where it's most satisfying and meaningful. That's where we find the most joy. That's the way God created relationships, and that's the way God created us.

THE ULTIMATE LESSON

God made men and women to be different from each other. Most of the time we're pretty happy about that. But sometimes those differences make it challenging to have and sustain a great sex life. Why is that? Is God cruel? No. We believe that God wired men and women differently so that we can appreciate the mystery of sex and so that we can continue to learn about each other.

Yes, sex is about pleasure, but so often we miss the larger purpose of sex. We seek immediate gratification, immediate pleasure. Sex is about *me*. Yet, that is the opposite of the way God works—and the opposite of the way God wants *us* to work, especially in our marriages and intimate lives. Ultimately this realization calls us to redefine sex.

We have brought into our bedrooms so many expectations and perspectives that shouldn't be there. We've listened to our culture for far too long; we've defined sex in ways that are displeasing to God.

The more the two of us work with couples who struggle sexually, the more frustrated we become at what Christians have allowed our culture to dictate about what should and should not happen in the bedroom. That's when we look at each other and determine that enough is enough. As Christian couples, we need to guard our bedrooms and our marriages. We need to cordon off our marriages from negative influences. We need to redefine the environment in our bedrooms and reestablish God's design for our sex lives.

ARE *You* CHEATING?

One day Pete called and in desperation asked if he and his wife, Cheryl, could make an appointment to meet Gary for counseling that day. When they arrived, Pete poured out their story. Earlier that day, while checking his e-mail at home, he'd found a message from one of Cheryl's male high school friends. This friend wrote about the time he had spent with Cheryl at a recent reunion. Pete then found a sexually explicit message of an upcoming rendezvous Cheryl was planning with this man. Pete learned that this man had already had a sexual relationship with Cheryl—something that should have belonged to Pete alone.

After listening to Pete, Gary asked him, "What do you want to do?" Because Cheryl had been involved sexually with another man, Pete had biblical grounds to be released from the marriage if he chose to divorce her.

Pete looked at Gary and said, "I have never cheated on my wife." But then after a moment, he turned to Cheryl and said, "I've never committed adultery. But, Cheryl, if I'm honest with myself, I have to confess that I *have* cheated you. I've been a workaholic. I haven't tended to your needs. I haven't cared for you the way you needed me to. I've cheated you—and I've cheated myself."

If you're honest, perhaps you're a lot like Pete: You're cheating your spouse. Before you deny it, think again. You may not be physically cheating through adultery or pornography, but you may be cheating your marriage out of the God-honoring, God-designed sex life that was meant for you and your spouse.

We cheat when we withhold affection, when we give too much of our time and energy to our kids or to others besides our spouses. We cheat when we connect emotionally with opposite-sex friends or colleagues. We cheat when we do not fully give ourselves sexually to our spouses. We cheat when we become selfish with our sexuality, when sex or the lack of sex becomes more about *me, me, me* than *we, we, we.*

Cheating is serious business to God. When we cheat, we do not simply hurt our spouses; we hurt ourselves, our marriages, and our relationship with God.

It's far easier to blame someone or something other than ourselves when our sex lives aren't all we know they should be. But we need to ask ourselves honestly, How are we cheating ourselves out of a successful and satisfying sex life? How are we cheating ourselves individually? How are we cheating ourselves relationally, physically, and spiritually?

Is it by fantasizing? Is it withholding a part of our hearts out of fear of becoming too vulnerable or getting hurt? Is it because of a spiritual hole we've never filled? Is it that we are not fully present when we make love to our spouses because we're thinking about other things instead?

These are all ways we cheat. Redefining sex means we face our selfishness head-on and admit: I am selfish, and my selfishness is cheating me—and my spouse—out of a great sex life. My selfishness is cheating me out of developing the character qualities that God wants me to have.

Redefining sex means we face our selfishness head-on.

When it comes to sex, we all want the climax, the grand finale. So if we don't reach an orgasm complete with earthquake and fireworks, we think that something must be wrong with our technique or the timing—or our spouses. Instead of pointing fingers at these factors, we need to redefine sex so that our focus is not on our own needs but on our spouses' needs, desires, and wants.

Good sex is other-centered; it allows you to focus solely on your spouse. God's design is that when you focus on your spouse's needs and he or she focuses on yours, your sexual and relational pleasure will be so deep that you won't want to do anything to diminish it.

Good sex is other-centered; it allows you to focus solely on your spouse.

Our sexual intimacy is tied to our faith. God created us with a purpose, and we want our lives to count. At the end of our lives we will give an account to our Creator, and our accountability is going to include the area of sex. We don't want to stand in front of God and hear him say, "I had this beautiful plan, and you missed out." When we realize this, we need to ask ourselves, Is my cheating really worth what I will get out of it? And what I will ultimately lose?

Sex Is a Privilege and a Duty

Monica and Hank sat across from Gary with their arms crossed. They were both sure they were right and the other was wrong. It seemed that every problem they had was the other person's fault. Finally, Gary broached the subject of sex.

Monica rolled her eyes and sat quietly. Hank looked bitter as he stated, "We haven't had sex in months."

Monica turned on him. "Gonna blame that on me, Hank? Well, no way. Our not having sex is not my problem."

"Why do you say that, Monica?" Gary asked, trying to restore some calm in the room.

"Why should I give him sex when he doesn't even try to meet any of my needs?"

"That's not true," Hank shot back. "I tried to meet your needs, but it was never good enough."

"When, Hank? You come home and don't lift a finger, except to flip the channels on TV. You treat me like a maid. You don't talk to me, except when you need me to get you a refill on a drink. Is that meeting my needs?"

"Well, if you were a little nicer, maybe I'd be more willing. If you acted like you wanted to have sex once in a while—"

"You are so unbelievable!" she said.

"Okay, hold off, you two," Gary said. He had worked with Hank and Monica in counseling long enough to know it was time for some tough talk about their sex life. "Monica, Hank, I have some things to say, and they may be difficult for you to hear. But part of my job is to tell you truth, to spotlight areas where you are struggling, and to hold you accountable in those areas. This isn't about you personally. This is for the sake of your marriage."

Gary had their attention, even if they gave it grudgingly.

"When you married, God called you into a mysterious and unique relationship—a relationship in which you complete each other, in which two people become one through the physical and emotional intimacy of sex. As a husband and wife, you are called to serve each other, and that includes the privilege and responsibility of satisfying each other's sex needs. That is a need only you can fully meet for the other, and that need is part of

God's will for you and your marriage. Satisfying each other's sex needs may feel more like a duty for you right now, but it is a duty God is calling you to respect.

God called you into a mysterious and unique relationship—

a relationship in which you complete each other, in which two people

become one through the physical and emotional intimacy of sex.

"Monica, for your husband, the physical act of intercourse is an important and fundamental part of sex. You may not like that, but that's the way it is. That is the way God created your husband. So it is part of your responsibility to fulfill that. If you don't, something or someone else will. And the tears may flow, but you will bear part of that responsibility. If the physical is not part of it, then you don't have a sexual relationship. And in God's view, you really don't have a marriage. That's not what God intended.

"Hank, for your wife, the physical part is not going to work if the emotional and relational parts of your marriage aren't working. You may not like that, but that's the way it is. That is the way God created your wife. So it is part of your responsibility to fulfill that. If you don't, something or someone else will. And the tears may flow, but you will bear part of that responsibility. If the emotional and relational are not part of it, then you don't have a sexual relationship. And in God's view, you really don't have a marriage. That's not what God intended. Sex is part of a larger picture. A healthy sexual relationship grows out of your emotional and spiritual relationship with your wife."

That was tough talk for tough love. But Hank and Monica needed to understand the seriousness of a marriage commitment. They needed to recognize that part of their commitment is to be emotionally, relationally, and sexually available to each other.

Gary sent them home with an assignment. For the next week, they were to focus on meeting their spouse's top need—without complaint, without a negative attitude. And he asked them to practice being grateful that they *could* meet that need. For Hank, it was to connect emotionally with Monica and to help around the house. For Monica, it was to respond in a positive way to Hank's sexual advances.

Within one week they began to see a change in their marriage. All because they acknowledged their cheating mentality and redefined their relationship.

Is It Ever Okay Not to Have Sex?

At a recent conference one woman asked us, "Is it ever okay not to have sex? How about when my husband and I are both stressed? What should I do when he asks me if we can have sex later and I am not feeling at all in the mood? I want to be a good wife, but I don't know how to handle those situations in a biblical way."

We receive similar questions from husbands: "I work hard all day and am exhausted when I get home. Does God really expect me to focus energy I don't have on being relational? Sex isn't difficult for me, but talking is! What should I do when I don't have anything to talk about?"

Is it ever acceptable to refuse to meet a spouse's sex needs? What does the Bible say about such situations? At one point the apostle Paul discusses sexual responsiveness: "The husband should fulfill his wife's sexual needs, and the wife should fulfill her husband's needs. The wife gives authority over her body to her husband, and the husband gives authority over his body to his wife. Do not deprive each other of sexual relations, unless you both agree to refrain from sexual intimacy for a limited time so you can give yourselves more completely to prayer. After-ward, you should come together again so that Satan won't be able to tempt you because of your lack of self-control."[1]

Paul is making several things clear. First, sex has an equality and reciprocity to it. Each spouse has the responsibility to satisfy the other. Paul challenges us not to withhold sex from each other because joining together in sexual unity blesses the other. Second, celibacy within marriage is not a good choice. A Bible commentary about this passage makes these observations about the historical practice of celibacy: "Apparently this refraining from sex within marriage was a unilateral decision of one partner, not a mutually agreed on decision. Such a practice sometimes led to immorality on the part of the other mate. Paul commanded that they stop this sort of thing unless three conditions were met: (a) the abstention from sexual intercourse was to be a matter of *mutual consent* on the part of husband and wife; (b) they were to agree beforehand on a *time* period, at the end of which normal intercourse would be resumed; (c) this refraining was to enable them to *devote* themselves *to prayer* in a concentrated way."[2]

The Bible's guidelines are designed to move us past withholding sex from our spouses unless both spouses agree for a time and they do it for the purpose of spending more time in prayer. If they don't agree or if the period of abstinence is for an indefinite period or if the purpose is something other than prayer, then they misunderstand God's design. We must never use Scripture as a weapon of control. The Bible is for our protection and benefit. In those times when a couple are committed to seek God in concentrated prayer, fasting, and searching the Bible for direction and comfort, taking time and attention for sex could diminish the search. But when they reconnect sexually, it will be richer because of the spiritual connection they have had with God.

Occasionally a couple may need to refrain from sexual intimacy because of a deep hurt. This often happens when one spouse is dealing with the effects of severe trauma, such as childhood sexual abuse or a partner's addiction to pornography. We'll talk more about these issues in chapter 13.

Becoming one in body and spirit leads us to meet each other's needs willingly. We give to each other out of a desire not only to experience sexual satisfaction but also to enrich the marriage. In other words, a successful sex life means we strive to serve our spouses.

"Before I truly understood what it meant to serve Candy, I would do kind things and expect something in return," James told Gary. "If I went grocery shopping, I counted on sex later that night. Even though my expectations were left unstated, I had an underlying hope that Candy would reciprocate." James's relationship with Candy changed when he redefined sex and began to serve his wife and meet her needs.

True service means persistently watching for ways we can love, assist, support, praise, appreciate, protect, and please our spouses—then taking action, *without* expecting something in return. That's not always easy. Opportunities to serve may come at inconvenient times, sometimes when we're not in a serving mode. We need to have the mind-set that sex isn't about me and my desires. Sex is about serving my spouse, whom God has given me.

True service means persistently watching for ways we can love, assist, support, praise, appreciate, protect, and please our spouses— then taking action, *without* expecting something in return.

Part One

THE FIVE SEX NEEDS
OF HUSBANDS AND WIVES

CHAPTER 3

What Spouses Need from Each Other

If you're married, we're sure this will come as no surprise to you: Men and women view sex differently. Very differently.

This is the stuff of *Cosmo* magazine articles, multitudes of books, television sitcoms, and stand-up comedy. The television sitcom *Everybody Loves Raymond* was a hit precisely because the writers understood the profound differences between the sexes and exploited those for comedy's sake. We are bombarded with that message so often, however, that many spouses start to tune it out, shaking their heads and mumbling, "Yeah, yeah, I know. We're different."

In some areas of marriage, our differences don't matter that much. Husbands and wives may have different styles of communication or may enjoy different hobbies. But because our sexual involvement touches us at such a deep level, the differences can sometimes be a source of conflict.

It's important to remember, though, that God intentionally made males and females to be different from each other. And we need to celebrate those differences. Our lives would be quite different if males and females looked alike, were shaped alike, thought the same way, felt the same way, and responded the same way. Our differences add richness and diversity as well as excitement and joy to our marriages.

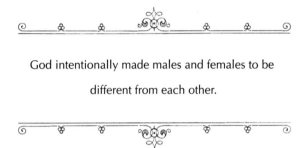

God intentionally made males and females to be different from each other.

However, our differences also create challenges. We need to learn what those differences are and understand how to navigate them in our unique marriage relationships.

We know that our brains and sexual organs are wired differently. Men are aroused by visual stimuli; a husband can just look at his wife and become aroused. Women are a little more complex. They need to be "warmed up." Sex therapists and researchers tell us that women take as long as thirty minutes to become aroused during sex. You've probably heard the metaphors that compare men's and women's sexual responses to microwaves and Crock-Pots.

Studies suggest that men think about sex every seventeen seconds, but women think about sex every seventeen days—or seventeen years, in some cases![1] Although these statistics highlight the extremes, they do point out a distinct difference, and the truth is, that difference is not going to change. Women just haven't been wired to think about sex as frequently as men do, but that doesn't make women prudes. Men have been wired to think about sex often, but that doesn't make them perverts. But we know that already, right?

If, in fact, our distinct wiring is such a commonly understood issue, if we know so much about why we are wired so differently, why is it still a problem in so many marriages? Why do husbands and wives forget and act as if this is breaking news—or bad news? And why do we continue to allow these differences to keep us from having strong sexual relationships?

GENDER WIRING 201

In our work counseling couples, we have found the problem is not that couples don't know about gender differences. The problem is that even though we recognize the differences, many of us never take the time to study, appreciate, and pursue those differences as being good and worthy.

Even though we recognize the differences, many of us never take the time to study, appreciate, and pursue those differences as being good and worthy.

Instead, many couples continue to assume that the wife will respond like a husband, and the husband will respond like a wife. Here's the Golden-Rule mentality again: If I treat my spouse the way I want to be treated, then we'll be happy and have a fulfilling sex life. This is one of the great misunderstandings of all time. If you've bought into that line of thinking, let us remind you: That is *never* going to happen. Period. It's that simple.

So what should a couple do? Should they resign themselves to experiencing a boring—or nonexistent—sex life?

No!

In our own marriage, whenever we have taken the Golden-Rule approach, we've bumped up against our differences. But those times are great reminders to learn about and appreciate the differences in each other. God made us different, but he also made us to be complementary—to balance each other, to fit together, to make us one.

The exciting reality about sexual intimacy is that God made us different to spice things up! And ultimately, those differences teach us about serving the other person. When we give our spouses what they *need*—not what we *think* they want or need—then we fulfill God's design for sexual intimacy. And the reward is that together we experience true intimacy.

When we give our spouses what they *need*—not what we *think*

they want or need—then we fulfill God's design for sexual intimacy.

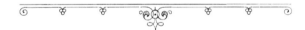

What we have to realize is that our different ways of approaching sexual intimacy are okay—and normal—because God made us different . . . on purpose. And that's a good thing. We waste so much time and energy trying to shape our spouses into sexual clones of ourselves. Then we wonder why we're frustrated and disappointed with our sex lives! So rather than growing frustrated and upset, taking it out on each other, walking away, and pouting, take those opportunities to accept that our approaches to intimacy are going to be different.

The reality is that we often want the same things. Our deepest desire, whether we're male or female, is ultimately to become one. He wants intercourse; she wants intercourse. He may want physical intercourse more than she does, and she may want emotional intercourse more than he does, but when a couple can meld physical and emotional intercourse, they will find the pathway to great sex.

To meet our needs, we have to meet our spouses' needs. They are ultimately connected. Of course, that's not to say that men *only* want the physical and women *only* want the emotional. Both need both. It's just that God wired us to get both by coming at it from two distinct ways.

So how did God do that? He wired a man to feel connected to his wife by experiencing orgasm. The physical act of sex opens his feelings and allows him to become more vulnerable. Sex gives him a sense of closeness and intimacy. He is better able to concentrate on such things as his emotions. God wired a woman to feel connected to her husband by experiencing emotional connection. Emotional connection gives her a sense of safety. She is better able to give herself to physical sex.

God made husbands and wives to complement each other: A husband invites his wife into intimacy through sex, and a wife invites her husband into intimacy through emotional connection. Together, they make a satisfying whole.

Ultimately, through sexual intimacy (emotionally and physically connecting), God calls us to be vulnerable and to serve each other. He calls on men to connect emotionally with their wives in order to have their physical needs met; he calls on women to connect physically with their husbands in order to have their emotional needs met. It involves tension, to be sure. But it's also exciting foreplay!

What Do Husbands and Wives Really Need?

So we know that men are visually stimulated and can become physically aroused fairly simply and quickly. We know that women are more complex and need emotional, physical, relational, and spiritual alignments to become physically aroused. But what exactly are our sex needs? If husbands and wives were to sum up what they wish their spouses understood about their sexual needs, what would be on their list of top five needs?

To help us understand the unique sex needs of men and women, we surveyed more than seven hundred married couples across the country. The results surprised and impressed us:

TOP FIVE SEX NEEDS OF MEN AND WOMEN

Men's Sex Needs	Women's Sex Needs
1. Mutual satisfaction	1. Affirmation
2. Connection	2. Connection
3. Responsiveness of wife	3. Nonsexual touch
4. Initiation of wife	4. Spiritual intimacy
5. Affirmation	5. Romance

Which of the results surprise you? Which ones line up with the needs you listed after doing the exercise in chapter 1? Again, don't be concerned if your lists don't match the results of our survey.

As you read the next four chapters about the top five sex needs of men and women, you will grow in your understanding of your own sex needs, your spouse's sex needs, the obstacles that may prevent you from meeting those needs, and practical ways to start meeting your spouse's unique needs.

Regardless of where you and your spouse are now, when you become serious about meeting each other's sex needs, you will see change in your relationship. It may not happen the first time you connect emotionally with your wife or the second time you initiate sex with your husband. But a willing persistence and a good attitude will bring about positive change. It simply takes commitment.

Before you jump in, however, consider these three things:

1. Think about your commitment level. How willing are you to doggedly pursue meeting your spouse's sex needs? If you think, *I will if he will,* then you'll see some changes, but you'll constantly be trying to balance the scale. And although you may experience sexual fulfillment for a while, you won't sustain that level of enjoyment and peace.

You may think, *Why should I be the one who has to work? That's not fair!* You're right—if you're thinking short term. But fulfilling your spouse's sex needs requires long-term thinking. And somebody needs to make the first move. If you both stubbornly refuse to initiate a change, then you'll stay stuck.

Or you may think, *What's in this for me? What if I meet my spouse's sex needs, but he or she doesn't meet mine?* Even though you may not initially feel as if your needs are being met, the more committed you are, the more you will see your spouse begin to soften and be willing to meet your needs.

2. Talk to your spouse. Pick a date night, take this book, and discuss the sex needs with your spouse. Ask questions and genuinely listen to the answers. The goal is not to persuade your spouse or to express why you don't see things his or her way. Your goal should be to learn and understand your spouse's needs from his or her point of view. Remember, your spouse's answers are not an invitation to debate your differences. Once you've listened, restate your spouse's answers to make sure you have heard and understood correctly.

If you've never talked together about sex, now is a great time to start. We think that talking together about your sex life is so important that we've devoted chapter 10 to the subject. But for now, tell your spouse that this topic is so important to you that you are willing to step outside your comfort zone to talk about it. Talking about sex needs can be draining, so don't push too much information into one discussion. Set up another date night to continue your discussion. If you need ideas about date nights that will help you discuss your sex needs, see chapters 6 and 11 in our book *40 Unforgettable Dates with Your Mate.*

DISCUSSION STARTERS

Not sure how to begin talking about sex? Begin by asking these questions:

- *What are your top five sex needs?*
- *What do these needs look like in our daily lives?*
- *If you would want me to meet one thing from your list next week, what would it be?*
- *How would it make you feel if I were to meet that need— and others—consistently?*
- *How can I serve you in meeting your sex needs?*
- *Is there anything you absolutely hate about sex?*
- *What makes you uncomfortable about sex?*

CHAPTER 4

A Wife's Top Three Sex Needs

How's Jeff?" Barb asked her friend Annie over lunch one afternoon.

Annie paused. "Okay, I suppose."

"What do you mean?"

Annie sighed. "Honestly? We're not doing so well. When we first got married, Jeff was so attentive. He'd constantly tell me I was beautiful. We held hands. He'd bring me flowers or call me at work just to tell me he loved me. We even prayed together every morning before we got out of bed. And the sex was wonderful!" She paused again. "Now we barely speak to each other."

Annie blinked back her tears. "I'm not even sure when we started to become disconnected," she continued after a moment. "I just know that we started to argue about sex. Jeff is always ready to go. The wind could blow, and he'd think that was foreplay. He doesn't understand that I'm just not that way."

"Most women aren't that way!" Barb said, trying to console her friend.

"Yeah, well, he doesn't even bother anymore—with sex, with

our relationship, with anything. What's worse, he won't talk about it."

Annie's story is similar to the hundreds we hear as we talk to women all across the country. They long to have a solid relationship with their husbands, but the sex part—at least the way they feel that their husbands view it—keeps getting in the way.

When we surveyed more than seven hundred women, we discovered they do want sexual intimacy. They want a great sexual relationship with their husbands. As we looked at the wives' top three sex needs, we realized the needs are closely interwoven.

Barb's conversation with Annie summed up the top three sex needs for most women: affirmation, connection, and nonsexual touch. Notice that her husband used to do the following things: He told her she was beautiful (affirmation); he would pray with her every morning and call her during the day (connection); they held hands (nonsexual touch).

Husbands, if you want your wife to desire you sexually and initiate and enjoy sex with you, it's important to understand that a mutually satisfying sexual relationship doesn't just happen. The good news is that if you understand one of these sex needs, you will more than likely grasp the others too. It takes work—but the benefits are worth it.

Let's take a look at each of the three sex needs.

Affirmation

During a recent conversation Jody told us, "Every once in a while I need to know that my husband recognizes and affirms what I do for him and our family. When I hear him say 'Thank you' or 'You did a good job' or 'You are such a good mother,' I feel closer to him and am much more open to his physical advances."

Affirmation is essential to a successful sexual relationship. It is so important that 65 percent of the women we surveyed rated it as their number one sex need.

So what exactly is affirmation? Simply put, affirming your wife means building her self-esteem. It's giving her genuine compliments, actively listening to what she says, giving her the opportunity to slow down from her busy pace of life, saying complimentary things about her in front of other people, and encouraging her when she's discouraged. Affirmation is pointing out what she does right, overlooking her failures, and reminding her how much you appreciate what she does.

Affirmation is especially important during sex. Women need to hear how beautiful they are and how much they satisfy their husbands. The truth is, a majority of women struggle with body image. It doesn't matter how old or how fit they are, they are always comparing themselves to other women or to themselves at their best form—which may have been when they were in high school. Why do you think women constantly ask, "Do I look okay in this? Do I look fat?"

CONNECTION

What a day Julia had. Several people had been laid off from her department at work—one of them a friend. The project she had hoped to finish that day was delayed because a coworker dropped the ball. Julia's mother had called with bad news about a friend's health. When Julia arrived home, she was stressed, tired, and depressed. She pulled into the driveway and saw Ben working on his 1967 Ford Fairlane in the garage. She grabbed her briefcase and got out of the car.

"Hey, sweetie!" Ben called, as he wiped his greasy hands on a towel and walked toward her.

"Hi," she said blandly.

After he kissed her, he asked, "How was your day?"

"Horrible," Julia said.

"That's not good. I'm sorry to hear that. Let's talk about it over dinner." And with that Ben kissed her again and went back to the garage.

As Julia walked into the house, she thought about how much she loved and appreciated Ben. Every night it was the same routine: He'd stop what he was doing to kiss her and ask, "How was your day?" Then he'd say, "Let's talk about it over dinner." During the meal they would share the events of their day and unwind together. Then later in the evening they would snuggle together on the couch and watch the news.

In the book *The Case for Marriage: Why Married People Are Happier, Healthier, and Better Off Financially,* sociology professor Linda Waite and marriage expert Maggie Gallagher conclude that married people have better sex. They suggest that "the lifelong, permanent commitment embodied in marriage itself tends to make sex better."[1] They also believe that "there is no better strategy for achieving great sex than binding oneself to an equally committed mate."[2]

That's exactly what women across the country told us. More than 59 percent of the women ranked connection as a top sex need. One key to a wife's sexual excitement, responsiveness, and ability to initiate sex is a strong connection to her heart.

These women feel that their sex lives are satisfying when both partners receive first an *emotional* and/or *spiritual* connection and then a *physical* connection. In other words, when a husband emotionally connects to his wife, he prepares her for sexual intimacy.

Women need physical closeness, but for them it doesn't start there. They first need emotional closeness. Julia and Ben have a great sex life. Why? Because Ben understands the importance of tending to his wife's needs. He stops what he is doing to greet her with a kiss. He asks about her day. He listens to her. He is physically close to her while watching television. And even when she is tired and stressed, because he has taken the time to bond with her, which helps her unwind, she is more available to meet his—and her own—sexual needs.

Ben understands that connection happens 24/7. He knows that a compliment at 10:30 won't translate into sex at 10:35. He realizes that to meet his wife's needs, he needs to be in the moment, not emotionally and mentally "checked out."

Women need to experience an emotional connection with their husbands *every* day. Here is what women told us about the ideal ways to connect with their husbands:

- "I connect with my husband when he checks in with me, just to say, 'I love you, and I'm thinking about you.'"
- "I feel connected to my husband when he asks me how he can pray for me and when he shares with me what God is teaching him in his life."
- "We connect by touching and doing activities together, like hanging out doing chores, walking together in the

grocery store, watching television. It's mostly nonverbal, but it's just as powerful for me."

- "My husband and I take long walks or work out together and talk. That connects me to him."

God brings women and men into relationship in different ways. Through sex, men draw women into a physical relationship. Through connection, women draw men into an emotional relationship. We complete each other. We both end up with relationship, but we have different ways of inviting the other person in.

Through sex, men draw women into a physical relationship. Through connection, women draw men into an emotional relationship.

Christian sex therapists Clifford and Joyce Penner say it well: "For the woman, sex is a total-body and total-person experience. It's good for her when her husband attends to all of who she is, not just her sexual parts."[3]

NONSEXUAL TOUCH

Jimmy complained, "Every time I go to kiss Karen, she pulls away, then says, 'All you ever think about is sex. Can't you just kiss me without needing it to become foreplay?' What is her problem?"

"Picture this," Barb said. "It's nearing the end of the day. The unfolded laundry is piled high, screaming kids are hungry, dinner is boiling over, and Karen is thinking, *If I could get just fifteen minutes of quiet so I can balance the checkbook, I'd be finished with what I need to do, and then I can relax.* Then from out of nowhere you show up and plant a big, juicy wet one on her lips. It's the we've-got-ten-minutes-before-dinner-and-I'm-ready-for-some-sex kind of kiss."

"Yeah? What's wrong with that?"

"Nothing," Barb said. "But here's the difference between you and Karen. Karen's goal is to complete her to-do list. Your goal is Karen! Karen loves you, but when you pick inappropriate times to move toward sex, she sees you as a wall that's blocking her from finishing that list—the one she compiled at dawn and wants to complete before dinner. She's not opposed to sex; she's just not interested right then."

"But why can't she just let the list go until later?"

"Because that's not how a woman's mind functions."

Gary could see that Jimmy wasn't comprehending the point, so he chimed in. "What's your favorite sport?"

Jimmy looked confused. "Football."

"If you were playing a game of football," Gary said, "and you had a fourth down with ten yards to go, and your wife stood on the field directly in your path, how would you feel?"

"Blocked."

"Imagine that Karen is playing mental football, and she has control of the ball on a fourth down with ten to go. How do you think she'll respond to you if your kiss isn't just a kiss, but a move to block her from finishing her goal?"

"Yeah, okay," Jimmy admitted.

"*After* she makes the touchdown, she's ready to celebrate—with you."

"So my kiss was the tackle?"

"Sort of. The kiss wasn't the problem," Gary said. "The *type* of kiss was the problem. For Karen, the kiss needed to be simply an expression of adoration, with no strings attached. It could have been a great connection. But for you, the kiss was foreplay, part of the countdown to sex."

Jimmy's wife needed something most women need and desire: physical touch that does not lead to sex. They need to feel secure that every physical expression their husbands make isn't with the expectation of moving toward intercourse. In our survey, more than 59 percent of the women ranked nonsexual touch as a top sex need.

Guys, you may be thinking, *Wait a minute. What is nonsexual touch doing in a sex book?* Some of you may even be wondering, *Is there such a thing as nonsexual touch? Isn't most touch between a husband and wife* supposed *to lead to sex?* The answers are: plenty, yes, and no. Simply put, nonsexual touch, or affection, is intimacy in and of itself. It's not the means to an end. In many situations it *is* the end.

Nonsexual touch, or affection, is intimacy in and of itself. It's not the means to an end. In many situations it *is* the end.

"Touch me. Don't touch me." Have you ever had that experience with your wife? One minute she wants to be touched; the next minute she doesn't. No wonder men are confused! But men need to understand what *kind* of touch works well for a woman. More than 80 percent of a woman's need for meaningful touch is nonsexual. Most psychologists will tell you a vast majority of women appreciate and love a hug, a touch, a kiss, holding hands—any physical sign that they are special.

First, let's differentiate between nonsexual touch and foreplay touch. Nonsexual touch is loving affection. It may have the tone of sexual arousal "around" it, but the goal of nonsexual touch is not intercourse. Foreplay touch, on the other hand, leads to sexual intimacy for a couple. The problem is, to a man, touch is touch is touch. It all feels the same. But that's not the case for his wife.

During one of our conferences Jack approached us with a complaint. "After dinner, homework, and getting the kids to bed, my wife, Rachel, and I sat on the couch and watched a movie on television. I reached toward her and gently rubbed the back of her neck and played with her hair. She melted in my arms and asked me to hold her. I thought everything was going great, so I started to kiss her neck and move closer. And then she froze! She got mad at me and said she wanted to be held—but *that's all*. What does she mean, 'That's all'? I'll never understand her. I give her the nonsexual touch she wants, and that's where it ends."

Guys, stay with us here. We know it may be difficult for you to understand how an intimate touch can stay platonic. You start rubbing her shoulders, and you become aroused and think you've entered the sexual intimacy zone. She thinks she's just getting an affectionate shoulder rub. And when you start to make your move, she resists and pulls back.

What happened? Many men have felt "out on the sofa" relationally, when they long to be "in bed" with their wives. When men go from nonsexual touch (which, in Jack's case, let's be honest, was actually *sexual* touch) to trying to score— they won't. It's that simple. Some men keep trying this pursuit, keep failing, and keep shaking their heads in bewilderment.

The reality is that when you meet your wife's needs for affection, you refresh her weary spirit and help her relax. You give to her, which begins to replenish her energy. When you touch her without any expectation that you will end up between the sheets, she will feel much more secure with you and much more open to sexual activity later on.

But when you offer her touch that you think will move into the sexual intimacy zone, you could drain her spirit and push her over the edge. Why? Because if your wife is like most women, she spends her day meeting other people's needs—giving, giving, giving. She gets tired and drained. When her husband comes home and moves right into the "take" mode, she doesn't have anything to give. She's empty. And that means sex isn't going to happen for a long time. Your wife needs you to be a safe and nonthreatening place for her. Nonsexual touch refuels her energy and creates that place of safety. Yes, she really does want to meet your sexual needs, but she needs time to refuel. You can help her do that through tender affection with no strings attached.

Your wife needs you to be a safe and nonthreatening place for her.

In the apostle Paul's profound chapter about the qualities of love, he reminds us, love "does not demand its own way."[4] You can love your wife by putting aside your own needs, by not demanding your own way, and by serving her through affirmation, connection, and nonsexual touch.

For a woman, great sex happens in the context of being held, laughing together, feeling accepted, and sharing feelings. Emotional intimacy is intensely fulfilling for a woman. Although it does not replace her need for sex, her emotional need is *as intense as* her husband's physical need. When her husband fulfills her emotional need and sustains it through affirming her, hanging out together, and being affectionate, she feels replenished and safe, making it much easier for her to be open to sharing herself physically with her husband.

Tanya, a young mom, told us, "A man needs to know that an invisible switch needs to flip before his wife jumps in bed and becomes an excellent lover. I'm a stay-at-home mom, and I have kids hanging on my legs all day and am generally beat by the time my husband comes home at night. I start my day with mundane things like potty training the kids, and I'm supposed to end it being intimate with my husband? Honestly, if my husband has sex in mind for later, I need a lot of affection before I can even think about that. He needs to invest in me before sex happens. When he calls home during the day, I feel connected to him. When I get a kiss on the cheek before the day starts or a warm hug after he comes home from work, he is investing in me."

UNDERSTANDING A WIFE'S NEED FOR AFFIRMATION, CONNECTION, AND NONSEXUAL TOUCH

Why are these three sex needs—affirmation, connection, nonsexual touch—so important to women?

1. They help build trust. Negative attitudes, doubt, insecurity, fear, guilt, and anger will kill sexual desire fast. But affirmation, connection, and affectionate touch can battle these emotions and help a couple bond. For a woman, trust is an essential foundation to a healthy sex life. Lyda told us, "I can't give myself fully to my husband if I don't feel safe with him, if I don't trust him. Trust and security allow me to let go and give my heart and body to my husband."

2. They help her want to please her husband. Several years ago a survey asked what employers could do to motivate their employees. The employers were amazed that the number one response had nothing to do with income or benefits; the workers said they needed appreciation.[5] If affirmation and appreciation motivate people to work harder, why wouldn't they motivate a wife to try harder to meet her husband's needs? The answer is, *they will.* Gratefulness expressed through affirmation and connection is a powerful motivator.

Although a man needs little or no preparation to engage in sex, a woman needs time to be emotionally and mentally prepared. That's why it's so important for a husband to meet his wife's sex needs in preparing her for sexual activity. When you ask about your wife's day, when you are concerned about her health, when you thank her for all the work she does, when you tell her she looks nice—her heart softens toward you. This is her foreplay. She naturally wants to be close to you physically.

3. They rev a woman's sexual motor. Believe it or not, meeting your wife's need for affirmation, connection, and nonsexual touch primes her sexual desire. Your nonsexual touch makes her feel loved for who she is—not for her body, not for what she is physically able to give you—but because you love her enough to put aside your own desire. When your wife feels loved, she will be more ready and willing to move toward you and meet your needs as well.

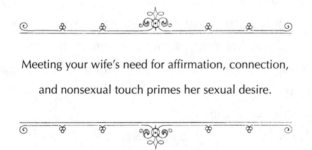

Meeting your wife's need for affirmation, connection, and nonsexual touch primes her sexual desire.

4. They melt tension and stress for both spouses. Touch is a powerful messenger that communicates care and connection. Anyone who has been soothed by a massage or comforted by an embrace knows how powerful touch can be. Without a single word, touch reinforces a message of love, connection, and acceptance.

God created our skin with delicate nerve endings that release into our bodies positive and healthy chemicals: endorphins and oxytocin—"feel good" chemicals. Soft touches and warm embraces can set off tiny nerve impulses throughout the entire body. A simple caress on the back of the neck transmits a touch message to the brain through a network of more than 100 billion neurons. The brain receives and interprets the touch message and then stimulates the production and release of endorphins, which give a heightened sense of good feelings and well-being. Touch increases brain activity and heightens alertness. Touch affects hormones as well as sleep patterns.[6]

Touch benefits both the giver and receiver. Researchers found that some type A husbands could add up to two years to their lives if they would give their wives a long, gentle hug at the beginning and the end of each day.[7]

5. They lead to positive chemistry in your relationship. Experts tell us that couples who generously show physical affection for each other nurture a healthy bond of connection. Chemistry and the senses are closely linked, and one of the strongest senses is touch.

What is the chemistry in your relationship? Do you still feel a flutter in your heart when your spouse takes your hand? If not, you can change that. You can program your brain so that you experience chemistry with your spouse. Writer Norman Cousins noted that the human brain is the largest pharmaceutical house in the world. He maintained that no drugstore has as many chemicals, or combinations of chemicals, available as the human brain. If our brains have every chemical necessary for producing passion and attraction, we need only to discover the way to signal our brain to release a certain chemical into the bloodstream.

Chemistry alone is not enough to hold together a relationship over the long term, but without chemistry, a couple's relationship is fragile and vulnerable. If a woman is deprived of nonsexual touch in her marriage, she may gravitate toward a man who touches her arm when they talk or who hugs her.[8]

6. They keep her physically and emotionally healthy. Several years ago researchers at UCLA made an interesting finding: To be physically and emotionally healthy, the average person needs eight to ten meaningful touches from a loved one each day.[9] Various other studies confirm that tender touch strengthens not only emotional health—communicating genuine acceptance, security, and comfort—but also physical health—increasing life span and aiding bone growth.

MEETING HER NEEDS EVEN WHEN YOU DON'T FEEL LIKE IT

Josh stood in front of Gary in disbelief. "That sounds great. But the truth is, it's tough for me to affirm and connect with Megan when she'd rather go to sleep, spend time with the kids, or have personal time. It's a challenge when all I hear are comments such as, 'Why can't you take out the trash when I ask you?' or 'You never listen to me when I talk to you,' or 'I wish you were more romantic.'"

"You're right," Gary told Josh. "That is difficult. But love often requires that we do things that are not easy for us. God calls us to sacrifice for the sake of the other person. I suspect that if you started to meet Megan's needs for affirmation and connection and affection, she would soften toward you."

Family expert Gary Smalley tells of a husband who had a similar experience. His response to his wife brought a radical change:

A couple who constantly bickered decided to go a week without voicing any criticism. Each time either of them became irritated, they wrote it down and placed the "complaint" slip in a box. Saturday night finally arrived, and the husband decided to go first. He opened the box and began to read the dozens of little notes. His eyes reflected the hurt and disappointment in himself as he read her complaints. "You've been promising to fix the screen door for six months, and it's still not fixed." "You never put your socks in the dirty clothes." "I'm getting sick and tired of having to pick up after you everywhere you go."

Then it was her turn. She opened the box and pulled out the first slip of paper. She read it with a lump in her throat. The next note brought tears to her eyes. Picking up three more notes, she read them quickly and began to weep. Every note in the box read, "I love you." "I love you." "I love you."

Like many husbands, you may have been fooled into thinking that one day your complaints would finally remold your wife into the perfect wife. But unconditional love and tenderness, not complaints, can transform a cranky opponent into a humble, loving partner. The importance of affirmation and verbalizing your feelings is invaluable. When you compliment her, thank her, hug her close, and brag about her—something happens inside of her. Affirming your wife opens her heart to you, connects her heart to yours, and then draws her body and sexual desire to you. Only after your hearts meet can your bodies meet.[10]

It sometimes takes work to give your wife the connection and affirmation she needs. It takes thought to give her the kind of touch that is meaningful to her. It takes courage to speak words of love for your wife—especially if she disappoints you. It takes sacrifice and wisdom to put her value above your own. It takes creativity to show your appreciation for her. In the busyness of life and the stress of keeping the family rolling along, it may be difficult, but it's well worth it. Love your wife with all of your heart.

What Happens When a Wife's Sex Needs Are Not Met?

What are the consequences if you do not meet your wife's sex needs? When you do not make an effort to meet her needs, the price is more than just "no sex." When a woman feels disconnected from her husband, she feels threatened and may react in a number of ways.

1. She may feel disappointed. When a woman feels disconnected from her husband, she doesn't feel cared for, appreciated, or valued. She may go through the motions, but she feels empty. She certainly won't initiate sex. Tamra experiences disappointment every time she asks her husband about his day but he never asks her about hers. "It's a simple, polite thing to do," she told us. "I know if I were his buddy, he wouldn't treat me like that. He doesn't connect to me, yet he expects me to connect physically with him. I don't think so."

2. She may feel rejected. The first three months of Nancy's marriage were not what she expected. She anticipated togetherness, romance, and companionship, but her husband, Richard, was consumed by his job as a girls' softball coach. Flattered by being in charge and by the attention he received from the girls at the ball diamond, he spent his energy on his job, not his wife. At one point, Nancy felt so lonely and excluded that she left for the evening and hid in a refreshment stand not far from the ball field, hoping her husband would come to look for her. He didn't. Not only was his wife crushed, but their marriage suffered. They both paid a price for Richard's unwillingness to meet his wife's needs.

3. She may begin to doubt and mistrust. When a wife's needs are not met, her imagination can run away with her. She may begin to doubt that her husband loves, desires, and appreciates her. When she doubts his feelings, she may then start to doubt his intentions. Once that happens, trust can erode.

4. She may see her husband as selfish. Janie told us, "I need Brad to *show* me as well as *tell* me he loves me. When he doesn't do those little things—holding my hand in the car, kissing me while I'm cooking dinner, asking about my day—it tells me that he doesn't care about me anymore. I begin to feel that he is just self-absorbed." To protect herself, a wife may begin to justify her own selfishness. She may stop trying hard to be a good wife, concentrating more on being a good mother, daughter, employee, or friend. She may not care if meals are prepared every night, if the bathroom is cleaned, or if the laundry is done. She may not be as patient with her husband's shortcomings. She may not dress up for him or initiate sex or respond to his advances.

5. **She may become irritable and resentful.** A wife whose needs are not met may be more defensive with her husband and blame him for problems. Brenda told us how even little bits of connection calm her: "Recently my husband and I were at a conference. I was in a bad mood for the first few days because the guys there got all his attention and focus. For instance, he would sit at a table with them and not save me a spot. It bugged me—and I took it out on him by becoming irritable. But one night while we were sitting at a general session, he put his hand on my back and rubbed it. My irritability vanished, and I calmed down. That's all I needed."

6. **She may pull away sexually.** A disappointed wife may distance herself from her husband, trying to protect herself, her emotions and sensitive spirit. She may rebuff his advances, offering excuses. Her resistance may escalate to saying no on a regular basis. If she does have sex, it may feel empty for her. This is the case for Vickie, who has been married for forty years. To the outside world her marriage would look like a satisfying one. She would disagree. The only time her husband touches her, for instance, is when he wants intercourse. This pattern has robbed her of any pleasure sexually. "The minute he touches me, I freeze. I feel like an object for sex, not someone he likes and enjoys being with."

7. **She may pull away emotionally.** A wife whose needs are not met may disconnect or shut down emotionally. When Laurie

came to Gary for counseling, she would open up about her heartache and weep openly, longing for things to get better. When nothing changed in her marriage—her husband continued to ignore her pleas for affirmation and connection—something changed within her. About a year later, she sat in Gary's office with a stony face, no emotion, no tears. "I'm tired of pleading," she said matter-of-factly. "I'm done." The most distressing part was that at the root of everything was a simple solution: Her husband needed to affirm, touch, and connect with her.

8. She may try to punish her husband. It's a sad reality, but when a wife becomes frustrated and upset enough, she may resort to punishment. Punishment will often come in the form of ignoring him or withdrawing emotionally, relationally, and physically. Or she may attempt to control and manipulate her husband through sex. When a wife has been hurt or rejected by her husband, when he does not affirm or connect with her, she may become desperate enough to try to hurt him by withholding sex.

9. She may look elsewhere to have her needs met. We've counseled hundreds of women who have strayed from their marriages. And almost every time, the reason was because their husbands stopped connecting with them—talking, touching, complimenting. So they reached outside the marriage and found men who did.

Most sexual affairs begin with an emotional connection—sharing personal information, seeing each other regularly, laughing together, sharing problems about their marriages, or flirting. Shirley Glass, author of *Not "Just Friends,"* reports that "82 percent of those who had affairs started out being social acquaintances, neighbors, or workplace colleagues with their future affair partners. They never imagined that their friends and co-workers would become co-conspirators in secret love trysts."[11]

A continued close friendship with someone of the opposite sex very often becomes sexual—and threatening and painful to a marriage. Glass also reports, "Friendships that build on an emotional level before becoming sexualized are more apt to be experienced as a deep emotional attachment. In my clinical sample, 83 percent of women and 58 percent of men who had extramarital sexual intercourse said that they had a strong or extremely deep emotional attachment to the affair partner."[12] People go where they're appreciated.

One woman told us that when another man helped her put on her coat, his warm touch sent chills up her spine, making her sexually aroused. Another told us of how one man in her office always touched a certain place in her back to affirm her. She also became sexually aroused.

We once heard someone say, "The grass isn't greener on the other side; it's greener where it's watered." If you are not affirming and befriending your wife, who is? The reality is that a woman responds to the man who takes care of her heart. When a husband doesn't give his wife the affirmation she needs, he leaves her heart wide open for another man to connect with her.

A woman responds to the man who takes care of her heart.

How to Meet Your Wife's Sex Needs

The previous paragraphs are sober reminders of what can happen when a wife's needs are not met. We encourage you to invest in your wife. Love her. Meet her needs—for her sake and for the sake of your marriage. How can you do that? Pick a few of the following suggestions, and begin the process of meeting your wife's sex needs.

1. Be consistent. If you give affirmation only when your wife has done something right or performed well, you can actually cause more harm than good. Your wife will begin to feel as if your love is based on her performance. Instead, affirm *her.* Thank her for the things she does for you and the family. Welcome her advice and insight. Praise her attempts.

2. Affirm her "just because." Randomly say "I love you." Brag about your wife. A wife is deeply strengthened when she hears her husband express love and appreciation for her in front of others. Amanda told us, "The other day I heard my husband telling his mother what he loves about me. I felt so warmed by his love that later that night, when he was interested in some physical intimacy, I felt so confident in his love that I was interested too."

3. Make her feel beautiful. Airbrushed images, magazine covers, movie stars, and models suggest that only certain body shapes are beautiful. Your wife needs to hear you tell her that she's beautiful. When a wife feels confident about her body, she is more willing and eager to pursue and enjoy sex. Appearance (weight, body size, breast size) is a sensitive issue for women; it can make or break a great sex life. Never tease your wife about her body.

Sheila told us, "I was shocked when my husband looked at

me during a movie in the theater and whispered, 'You really are beautiful.'" If you think those kinds of thoughts about your wife, say it!

Some women have a difficult time accepting that their bodies are okay. Dani hated the way she looked. Ray felt that his wife's self-consciousness was irrational, so he said to her every day, "You're beautiful just the way you are." He even purchased a handheld mirror and painted the words "I am beautiful" on the bottom. He placed the mirror next to her bathroom sink. He asked Dani, "Do you love me?"

"Yes, you know I do," she said.

"Then I want you to pick up this mirror every time you come into the bathroom. I want you to look into it and read the words written on it. Even if you don't believe them, I want you to say them aloud. I want you to know that's what I think of you. I think you are beautiful—both inside and out."

Dani begrudgingly agreed to his request. Every time she went into the bathroom, she held up the mirror and repeated the words "I am beautiful." After a few weeks, she began to notice that she started to believe what she was saying. Not that she thought all of her was beautiful, but she started to notice that she had a nice smile. Then she began to like the way her hair sparkled with strands of silver. She decided that her breasts really weren't all that small; they were "just enough."

One day when Ray said, "You look beautiful," she finally smiled and said, "How would my wonderful husband like to make love to his beautiful wife?"

Ray addressed his wife's needs with persistence and love. And his choice paid off.

One man called in to our radio program and told us, "But I *do* think my wife is overweight and needs to lose some pounds. It's not attractive to me at all. I struggle to become aroused."

"That's an issue you need to deal with too," we challenged him. "Telling your wife that she needs to lose weight is the fastest way to make sure she *doesn't* lose the weight, and it is sure to kill your sexual intimacy, which will then kill other parts of your relationship."

If a wife knows or believes that her husband is not attracted to her—especially because of her insecurities about her body— she will disconnect from him. She will feel that his love for her is conditional. Part of a husband's responsibility in loving his wife "as Christ loved the church" is to affirm and encourage her.[13]

If becoming aroused is the issue, then make love to your wife with the lights off. Change body positions. If a husband wants to help his wife become more physically pleasing, then he can offer suggestions such as, "I'm in the mood to take a walk. Want to come with me? That way you can tell me about your day." It's connecting to her without criticizing her shape. Another option is to start affirming what *is* beautiful to you—her smile, her eyes, her breasts, her hands, her laugh, the way she wears her hair. Encourage your wife. Pray for her.

Make a list of ten physical things you like about your wife. Next to each item in your list, indicate how you intend to praise her in that area. Then for the next week, practice affirming and encouraging her.

4. Learn what's in her mind. For a woman, 99 percent of sex is in her mind. That's where sexual interest—or disinterest— begins. If a woman *feels* drop-dead gorgeous (even if she's not), she will perform sexually as if she is! Find out what your wife is battling: a friend's betrayal, a dissatisfying job, a critical mother, an angry or distant child, a job loss, depression. When a husband finds out what's going on inside his wife's head, he is better able to encourage her.

5. Include her in your life. Lee is a huge hockey fan. Although Emma is not as interested in hockey, she goes to all the games with him. "It's not really about the games," she says. "It's more about the fact that he asks me to go with him—and he really means it when he says he wants me with him. He could probably go with his brother and have a better time. But he chooses me. It puts me in his world." Invite your wife into your work world too. Your job is an enormous part of your identity, and your wife wants to know what excites and challenges you about that world. Share your successes and failures with her. She isn't asking so she can judge you; she's asking because she genuinely wants to be part of your life.

6. Make eye contact. Look into her eyes when she talks, and hold her gaze. "When my husband catches my eye and holds it when we're eating dinner," says Cassie, "I get tingles. It's as if the kids and their messes and noise don't exist. It's just the two of us." Use your eyes to flirt with your wife.

7. Verbally affirm her during sex. When a man talks to his wife during sex, he communicates to her that he is mentally present. The strongest way to make that connection is to describe what she means to you and how much you appreciate her. To affirm her appearance, tell her that you're enjoying her body. Then describe her body in beautiful ways. (Check out how Solomon described his beloved in the Old Testament book Song of

Songs.) Tell her how you love looking into her eyes because they're the window into her soul, and her soul is pure and beautiful. Tell her you love feeling her soft skin against yours. Tell her how shapely she is and that God gave her wonderful curves. Tell her she carries femininity better than any other woman you know. Tell her that you'd like to explore every nook and cranny of her body, just as an artist explores a masterpiece. Tell her that she smells good, that she tastes good, and that she feels good. Tell her she brings you pleasure; tell her what she's doing right. Get excited over her attempts to please you sexually. Remember, women are responders, so if you tell her that you're "into it" by affirming her, she'll be more into it too.

8. Stay close afterward. After you have enjoyed each other physically, affirm and connect to your wife by staying close and cuddling. Don't just roll over and say good night ("Wham, bam, thank you, ma'am"). Be tender. Bask together in the glow of making love in the way that only God could have created. Tell her how much you enjoy being married to her. She needs your verbal connection to bring closure.

9. Learn from her. Often a woman wants her husband to say something to connect with her after she's been hurt, exhausted, or exasperated—and that doesn't come automatically to most men. For example, when your wife feels hurt, you might be tempted to say, "You're a tough woman. You'll make it." But your wife may need comfort, not a pep talk. How will you know what she needs? Learn to ask her. This may sound forced or unnatural, but say, "What do you need me to say right now?" Your wife can teach and help you. She may say, "Honey, just ask me if I'm okay" or "Give me sympathy" or "I just want you to hold me." It may feel awkward at first to respond to what she says, but it's better than guessing and getting it wrong. You can joke about it, but realize that asking your wife and learning from her can be transforming. She will be encouraged by your open spirit and your desire to connect to her in a way she needs and prefers.

10. Identify her need and preferences for touch. To identify your wife's "touch tone," ask yourself these questions:

- How does my wife express touch to me most often?
- What does she request from me the most?
- What does she complain about? (Does she complain when you touch her too much, too little, too sexually?)
- Learn when your wife prefers the nonsexual hug and the sexual hug. The nonsexual hug says, "Way to go," "I'm proud of you," "I like you a lot." The sexual hug extends to erogenous zones and says, "You feel good. I'd like to explore more of you." There is a time for the sexual hug and a time for the nonsexual hug. Learn when your wife needs and appreciates both kinds of touch.

11. Ask her how you are doing. One evening when we were getting ready for bed, Gary became uncharacteristically serious. "Barb, am I meeting your need for nonsexual touch?" he asked. "Do I touch you enough?" I confess, the first thought I had was to use this question to get every back rub, hand rub, and foot rub that I could out of this man, but then I quit feeding the bad dog in me and answered him, "Hey, you're doing a great job." Understanding that he wanted to connect with me in that way made me much more eager to connect with him in a sexual way.

12. If you're confused, clarify. If you sense confusion in your marriage about nonsexual touch, then talk about it. Wives, you might say, "When you hugged me just now, I felt you were asking for more than just a hug. It felt like foreplay." Husbands, you might ask, "What kind of nonsexual touch do you need?" A relationship breaks down when a couple defines nonsexual touch from two different vantage points. It's better to ask and know exactly what your spouse is thinking than to try to read his or her mind, which can lead to conflict.

13. Schedule time for connection. Your wife needs a steady diet of appreciation, encouragement, "talk time," nonsexual touch, and help around the house. She will receive those if you use a system of reminders that works best for you. Guys, that may mean you literally write "help with the housework" on your daily planner.

Here are some suggestions for helpful things you can do at various intervals:

- **The first fifteen minutes you are together in the evening.** When you get together in the evening—whether one or both of you have been out at a job—take the first few minutes to connect. How you connect will either help you feel glad you're together again—or not. Avoid complaining and pointing out things that didn't get done. Make each other feel happy to be together again. The first fifteen minutes set the tone for the whole evening.

  Steve Stephens, author of *20 Surprisingly Simple Rules and Tools for a Great Marriage*, calls his wife, Tami, before he leaves work every day to let her know when to expect him and to see if she needs him to pick up anything on the way home. It's also to find out how every-thing is going. He writes, "When I call, I listen for Tami's stress level. Some evenings all is well. At other times, I hear a tone of voice that says, 'Get home as quick as you can because the kids are driving me crazy, and I'm not sure how much longer I can keep it to-gether.' Those are the nights I know Tami needs me ei-ther to bring home dinner or to take the kids out to McDonald's or give her a break by watching the kids while she gets out of the house."[14]

One night Steve came home, looked around at a messy living room, and said, "What have you been do-ing all day?" As soon as the tears formed in his wife's eyes, he realized he'd messed up big time, so he told her, "Excuse me. Let me try this all over again." He walked out of the house, drove around the block, and rang the doorbell again. When she answered, he put his arms around her, gave her a huge kiss, and said, "How could I be lucky enough to be married to the most beautiful girl in the whole world? I've missed you all day, and I am so glad to finally be home." Go out of your way to connect to your wife when you are together again at the end of the day.[15]

- **Every day.** Check in with your wife during the day if that is possible. When you are home, set aside some time to be alone together and do something you both enjoy: taking a walk, watching a video, playing a game, cooking, or talking while holding hands. Touch your spouse lovingly at least five times a day. Kissing, hugging, and holding hands are all healthy touches. "Couples who connect physically in some way every day will have sex more often and enjoy more pleasure when they do," write Clifford and Joyce Penner in *A Married Guy's Guide to Great Sex*.

- **Three times a week.** Ask your wife, "How can I help you? How can I ease your stress level?" Ask what you can do around the house. You'll really get her attention if you initiate helping with dishes or folding laundry. Taking on some of her commitments will lift a big load from her shoulders and free her energy to share sexually with you.

- **Every weekend.** Have a scheduled dinner with just the two of you. You can talk about anything except these three topics: children, finances, and hot-button issues. Instead, discuss what interests your wife. Be interested and interesting. And turn off the cell phone! (If you want ideas for discussion starters, see our book *40 Unforgettable Dates with Your Mate*. We include ideas for five different levels of interaction, from "Dip Your Toes into the Water" to "Diving in Head First.")

- **Once a month.** At this point, you may be wondering, *Where is the schedule for sex?* That's a fair question! Talk to your wife and ask if the two of you can count on one evening per week for sexual time to enjoy each other's bodies. Set aside a night once a month to try new ideas and add variety to your sex life.

CHAPTER 5

A Husband's Top Three Sex Needs

Everything okay, Jeff?" Frank asked his friend while they were playing a round of golf one Saturday afternoon.

"Hmm?" Jeff answered distractedly. "Yeah, fine."

"Well, you've smacked that golf ball into every sand hole in this place. You're playing a terrible game. What's the matter? Annie not giving you any?"

Jeff sighed. "It's a little difficult, considering her favorite word is *no*. We haven't had sex in months."

Taken aback, Frank muttered, "I was just joking, man. It's really that bad?"

Jeff took another swing at the golf ball. "Yep."

"Women," Frank said.

"I just don't get her," Jeff said. "When we first got married, we were all over each other. We couldn't get enough. Now, if I even *touch* her, she tenses up and acts like I'm some molester. She makes me feel like I'm a pervert."

In the last chapter we discussed the top three sex needs for women: affirmation, connection, and nonsexual touch. Now let's look at the three top sex needs of the nearly seven hundred men we surveyed: mutual satisfaction, connection, and responsiveness.

Do any of these surprise you? Women are often amazed that the number one need of the men surveyed is mutual satisfaction; they would have guessed the top need would have been sexual release. But the survey shows that although the physical act of sex is an important part of sexual intimacy for men, it is not the most important aspect. Men want fulfillment—for their wives, as well as for themselves. Note that one need—connection—is the number two need for both husbands and wives.

Just as the women's top sex needs are interrelated, the men's needs are also interconnected. They are all about relationship.

We'll explore these three needs and offer suggestions about how to meet them.

MUTUAL SATISFACTION

Discouraged by some of the things happening in his marriage, Brian arranged to talk with Gary. "I've never felt so alone," Brian said.

"Why do you say that?" Gary responded.

"Paula and I used to make love all the time. Then we started to go for long periods without sex. Now we just don't have it at all."

"When was the last time?"

"Eight months ago," Brian said.

"Why so long?"

"I don't know," Brian said. "For several months I waited for her to bring it up—to show some desire, that she missed having sex with me. When I finally mustered up the courage to ask her about it, she said, 'I just don't need it.' When I told her I did, she said, 'Well, I could lie there and let you do your thing.'"

"And did you do that?"

"For a while I did," he said, sounding almost ashamed. "I needed a release. But it was awful—for both of us. I don't want sex with Paula if she's not into it too. I need to know she's enjoying it as much as I am. I need to know that I'm pleasing her and that she's interested in pleasing me."

Brian is not alone in his frustration. A guy once told us his wife had told him, "If it weren't for sex, I'd love being married."

When we first started telling people about this book, many women said, "Five sex needs! I thought for men there was only one: Just do it!" Then when we informed them that our survey indicates that a man's top three sex needs are mutual satisfaction, connection, and responsiveness, the women were pleasantly surprised. One woman commented, "This really helps me. Tad and I don't talk about sex much, and I just assume that he is like most men I read about—ever eager for sex. Maybe his needs are deeper and more complex than I thought. I need to talk to him about this. Even if mutual satisfaction isn't his number one need, I would feel so relieved to know that he is as concerned about my pleasure as he is about his own."

Yes, men need a physical release. In fact, they not only want it, but they actually do need it. Testosterone builds in their systems, and they need to release it. Yes, they do think about sex a lot, but God also designed them with a strong desire to *need* their wives to enjoy the experience just as much as they do.

More than 67 percent of the men who responded to our survey listed mutual satisfaction as their top sex need. They indicated that they believe a good sexual relationship is one in which *both* husband and wife experience satisfaction during lovemaking.

A good sexual relationship is one in which *both*

husband and wife experience satisfaction during lovemaking.

Many couples do experience this balanced sexual relationship. With a glow in her eyes, Penny told us, "During the thirty-six years of our marriage, Brad has always made my pleasure—my coming to orgasm—his first priority. I can't remember a time when he insisted on his pleasure before mine. Not that I was always able to come to orgasm, but he is always so patient with me. I trust him and am deeply committed to his satisfaction too."

Brad offered these comments: "When I know Penny is enjoying our lovemaking, I am one happy guy. In fact, I get intensely aroused when I sense she is responding. I feel so fulfilled when I know I can give her pleasure." It's not hard to imagine that Penny and Brad have a fulfilling sex life.

Men often find it difficult to express their needs and fears. Even though a husband's behavior may suggest that he feels sex is all about him, on the inside he desperately desires to satisfy his wife just as much as he wants to feel satisfaction. That's why a man feels threatened when he thinks his wife is dissatisfied with their sex life.

Sexual satisfaction is more than simply a physical release for a man. The purpose of mutually satisfying sex is not just orgasm but satisfaction through an emotional and spiritual connection. In his book *Learning to Live with the Love of Your Life,* e-Harmony founder Neil Clark Warren writes, "A satisfying sex life is not totally dependent on having orgasms. While only 29 percent of women reported always having orgasms during sex, compared to 75 percent of men, the percentage of women and men who find their sex life 'extremely' physically and emotionally satisfying is about the same—40 percent."[1]

A man feels like a man when he can please his wife. Gary has found in his counseling that nearly half of a man's self-image is locked up in his sexuality; in some men it may be closer to 90 percent! A man often thinks, *Am I a good lover? Am I capable? Can I do it well?* Thus any man who hears his wife say "I could lie there and let you do your thing" will hear an internal resounding *no* to those questions and will feel robbed of his self-esteem.

A man feels like a man when he can please his wife.

Author Shaunti Feldhahn writes, "One man [told me]: 'Everyone thinks women are more emotional than men. And everyone thinks that when it comes to sex, guys just want to 'do it,' and women are more into the emotion and cuddling of it. So women think there are no emotions there. But there *are,* and when [wives] say no, [they] are messing with all those emotions.'"[2]

Wives, your husbands really want to give you pleasure. A friend of ours put it well: "All men like to think they are low-level superheroes. That doesn't stop when they walk into the bedroom." When a wife receives pleasure from her husband, he feels wanted. Their intimate sexual interludes affirm his masculinity. They say to him, "I love the things that make you a man."

When Natalie heard us talk about a husband's desire to please his wife, she responded defiantly, "Oh yeah? Then why does my husband reach orgasm, then roll over and go to sleep, never once worrying about my climax?" Although most men really want their wives to experience pleasurable orgasm, the unfortunate reality is that some husbands wrongly use their wives for sex. If a husband has sex just for the release, then the couple is probably experiencing other marital problems as well. Those men may be dealing with deeper internal issues. We'll take a look at some of those in later chapters.

CONNECTION

Steve was grilling burgers at their family's barbecue when his wife, Brandy, walked past him on her way to set the picnic table. She brushed hard against him. "Oh, excuse me," she said coyly. He looked up as she smiled and blew him a kiss.

A few hours later he glanced over at her while she was wiping ketchup off their son's chin. She winked at him. *I'm a fortunate man,* he thought.

Still later that evening, after everyone had gone home and he and Brandy had cleaned up, Steve put the kids to bed and walked downstairs to the family room to watch some television. Brandy walked past him, leaned down, and kissed the top of his head.

"Hey," he said as he reached up and grabbed her arm. "Sit down with me."

"I can't," she said. "I just have a few more things to finish before I can relax."

"Forget about that for now. I'll help you later. Come sit down."

"You promise you'll help?" Brandy said.

"Cross my heart."

"Okay, but if you don't, you're in big trouble."

He smiled as she sat down and nestled against him to watch television.

Steve kept his promise and helped her finish some of the chores; then they went to bed and made love.

Nothing makes men feel closer to their wives than being physically and emotionally connected. That is why 66 percent of men ranked connection as a top sex need. Connecting inside the bedroom is pretty clear-cut; it's sexual intercourse. Sex builds connection for a husband in the same way that talking and helping around the house build connection for a wife. It's that simple.

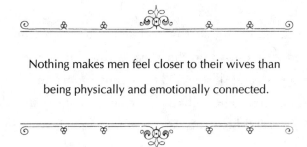

Nothing makes men feel closer to their wives than being physically and emotionally connected.

But Steve and Brandy were both physically *and* emotionally connected. When Brandy pushed Steve in a playful manner earlier in the afternoon, when their eyes met, when she winked at him, when she kissed the top of his head, and when the day culminated in lovemaking, she connected with her husband.

Most of those connections are not big energy expenditures. But they do take some thought. What are the simple things wives can do to say "You are important to me" or "You are a priority" or "I love you"? Touching his arm. Rubbing his back. Squeezing his shoulder when you walk by. Playing footsie or rubbing knees under the table. Holding hands. Putting a hand on his knee while you're in the car together. Meeting and holding his gaze. Blowing him a kiss. These are powerful ways a husband and wife connect. When a wife understands her husband's physical needs—both inside and outside the bedroom—she tells him clearly that she wants to connect with him.

Like women, men desire to be understood, listened to, accepted, cared for, encouraged, and given attention. This kind of connection occurs when a wife seeks to learn what's important to her husband: work, sports, his views, his often guarded emotions. When a wife connects to her husband in these ways, she shows not only the value she places on the relationship but also the value she sees in him.

One day last summer I (Gary) was watching a Cubs game. Barb had started to clean the house before our kids were to arrive for a visit, and she entered the family room and asked what I was watching. "The Cubs are playing. I want to catch the last two innings. I'll help you get ready for the kids' visit in a few minutes."

"Just watch the game," Barb told me. "I can pick up. I know you love the Cubs."

I have to admit, I was surprised when Barb said that. I don't usually mind helping her, but I really thought she wanted help *right then*. When she didn't, it made me look forward to spending time with her. I felt as if she understood me, that she had connected with me. After the ball game, I went into the kitchen to help.

Barb stopped wiping the counter and looked at me. "I've noticed you've been charging pretty hard lately. In the midst of all your work commitments, are you finding time to relax?"

The question threw me. She noticed my stress and cared about my well-being. Again, I felt a connection to her.

"Would you like to take a walk?" she asked.

"Now?"

"Sure," she said and dropped the cloth on the counter. "We can finish cleaning when we get back. Taking some time out is more important."

Even though the house wasn't completely cleaned and our kids were due to arrive soon, we took a break. As we went to our favorite walking path, Barb held my hand and asked questions about my work. When we sat on a bench, she rubbed my neck gently. I started to let down, inviting her into my thoughts. I shared how anxious I was feeling because of increasing work pressures. Barb listened with patience and concern, and we prayed. Then she suggested I take a half hour to relax when we returned home.

As we walked back to our house, I felt close to Barb. After the kids left that night, I couldn't wait to feel my wife physically close to me—and since we had emotionally connected, she was eager! That night we experienced a physical culmination of the mental, emotional, and spiritual connection that happened earlier in the day.

What did Barb do to set the stage for the trust and security that led us to a meaningful time of sex? She connected to my need to wrap up a baseball game that was of no big consequence, and she honored my need just to unwind for a half hour. She entered my world, listened, touched me, and encouraged me. The physical oneness we experienced further celebrated our love for each other.

Now, we're not suggesting that wives should allow their husbands to watch sports while they clean! At times Barb *does* need me to help right then, and I turn off the television and help. But in this particular situation, she recognized that I needed some downtime.

The reason why connection improves a couple's sexual relationship is that it increases a husband's emotional dependency on his wife. His attraction toward her will increase. He will laugh with her. He will find her idiosyncrasies attractive instead of annoying. He will accept her completely.

Openness and emotional trust keep people intimately united. Marriage therapist David Kantor says, "The raw sexuality and libido that come naturally with our biological inheritance are small and over time play a decreasing part in sexual intimacy. If that young desire is not replaced with deep sharing and receiving, then you really won't have an intimate life. But every time we connect on a deep level, we feel a need for sexual intimacy. There is something about being known and being received that is fundamental to the experience of desire."[3]

Openness and emotional trust keep people intimately united.

A study conducted by University of Washington psychologist and marriage researcher John Gottman found that emotional connection was the missing element in marriages that ended in divorce. Gottman and his team videotaped couples talking and interacting. At first the results seemed trivial—until the researchers noticed something: Couples were making bids—advances—for an emotional connection. Their responses to those bids determined the quality of their relationships. These emotional advances could come in the form of a question, a look, an affectionate touch on the arm, or any single expression that said, "I want to feel connected to you."

Gottman's research showed that husbands who eventually divorced ignored their wives' emotional advances 82 percent of the time, compared to only 19 percent for men in stable marriages. Women who later divorced ignored their husbands' emotional advances 50 percent of the time, while those who remained married disregarded only 14 percent of their husbands' bids.

Gottman and his researchers found that a typical happy couple may make up to one hundred bids over the course of the dinner hour. Think about your own relationship. How often do you try to make a connection with your spouse? How often do you ignore or reject your spouse's attempt to connect with you? According to Gottman, the satisfaction in your sex life is directly related to the frequency with which you initiate connection and respond to your spouse's attempt to connect with you. Wives, your husbands will feel honored, valued, and drawn to you when you bid for their connection, or when you respond to their bids. [4]

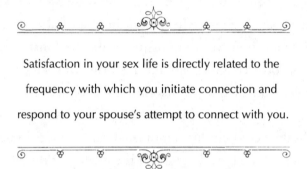

Satisfaction in your sex life is directly related to the frequency with which you initiate connection and respond to your spouse's attempt to connect with you.

Connecting to a husband's emotions isn't as easy as talking over a cup of tea with a girlfriend. Many men grow up with a sense that being strong and not showing emotion is the "masculine" thing to do. In his book *Connecting with Your Husband,* Gary Smalley writes, "When a male brain is saturated in testosterone, it doesn't take much, even from well-meaning family members, to give a boy the message that emotions and feelings are only for girls." [5]

Often men don't have the wide range of emotions that women do because men weren't reared to experience or express emotion. Once Gary's older brother, Jack, inadvertently hit him above the eye with a baseball bat. Gary remembers his brother's words: "Don't cry, and don't tell Mom!" His message? Don't *experience* emotion, and don't *express* it. Wives, although your husbands *do* experience emotion, they often express it in a way that doesn't make sense to you. So be patient with them. They want to experience and express emotion, but they often do not know how to do so appropriately.

Sometimes the best way to unlock a husband's emotions is through satisfying his physical needs for sex. Carrie told us, "I've been trying to connect to Phil's world for years, but he shuts me out. He won't let me in to what he's thinking." When men find themselves overly stressed, anxious, or facing loss, they crawl inside themselves for protection. They shut down to avoid conflict and talking. Yet doing the work to connect to what he is thinking and dreaming can bring a 180-degree change in him. And many times this happens through sex—the time when men let down their guard and allow themselves to become more vulnerable. We suggested to Carrie that rather than trying to force Phil to talk and share his feelings, she should focus on making herself available to him sexually, flirting with him, making sexual advances throughout the day.

Several weeks later, Carrie contacted us. "You aren't going to believe this," she said. "I did what you told me. I stopped prying and just began to focus on meeting Phil's sexual needs. Last night, he suggested we go for a walk, and he really opened up. He talked about what's going on at his job and how he feels as a result. We had one of the best conversations we've had in years."

"So sex was his connection, huh?" we said, trying not to laugh. We definitely *could* believe what she told us. Sexual release helps men become emotionally open.

Sexual release helps men become emotionally open.

What can frustrate a wife is having her husband pursue sex with her when she feels disconnected, angry, or preoccupied. Several wives have asked us, "How can my husband want sex with me when we're not connected?" The answer is this: A husband more easily connects with his wife through sex than by talking about emotions. He is more able to connect to her emotions and be sensitive once he feels safe and once his sexual needs are met. It's important for a wife to understand that sex is her husband's avenue to connection.

Wives, we want you to try an experiment. The next three times you have sex, set apart some time about thirty minutes after sex (if it isn't in the middle of the night) to start a conversation with your husband and test the waters. Is he more responsive? Does he tend to connect more? Our hunch is that most of the time the answer will be yes. After sex, men go through a resolution time of wanting to rest and shut down. This is primarily rooted in the physiological release and the body's desire to recuperate. But after thirty minutes or so, he is often very tender. Frustration diminishes, his mind will clear, and he may be more open to you.

RESPONSIVENESS

"Why doesn't she *ever* want to have sex?" Caleb asked Gary. "I do what I can to meet her needs. I know her plate is full. Before we had kids, she responded to me. She loved making love, lying around on Saturday mornings, and being with me. Now it's a big deal if I want to have sex. I'm not blind that she's tired with work, the kids, and all she has going, but when can I expect her to respond to my needs?"

When a wife rejects her husband's advances, he often interprets her lack of sexual response as "I don't care about you" or "Your needs are not important." Responsiveness is so important to husbands that nearly 63 percent of the men surveyed ranked it as a top sexual need.

When wives hear this, they usually ask us, "You mean I can never say 'Not tonight'?" Not at all. There are undoubtedly times when having sex just isn't going to work out. But it's important to understand what a lack of response will communicate. When a wife turns down a sexual advance, her husband feels emotionally rejected. And deep down, men are extremely sensitive. Many people think women are the sensitive ones. Although that's true, men are often even *more* sensitive, especially in the area of sex.

When a wife responds to her husband's sexual need, he feels loved. But when she ignores or overtly rejects this need, he feels unwanted and unloved. He is hurt by her frustrated looks, half-hearted attempts, and complaints.

Sex is a man's way of feeling close. When a wife rebuffs or ignores his sexual advances, she sends the message that she doesn't want to be close to him. Some of you wives may be shaking your heads, thinking, *That's not what I mean when I don't jump at every sexual touch or wink.* You're right. Even though your husband may know in his head that you don't mean to communicate that message, in his heart he finds it difficult not to believe that.

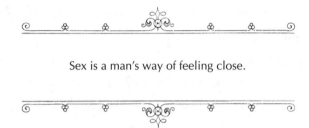

Sex is a man's way of feeling close.

One of the greatest threats to a husband's sense of worth is his sexuality. After a wife says "Not tonight," his mind may fill with irrational thoughts: *She cares more about the kids than about me. I'm a waste of time to her. Her to-do list is more important to her than I am. Maybe I'm just a poor lover.*

Most of you wives know the power of this kind of irrational thinking. You battle with it as well. When your husband makes a sexual advance and watches for your answer, he wants you to *want* him.

In his classic book *Love Life for Every Married Couple,* Ed Wheat writes, "The husband greatly desires response from his wife. She can give him this beautiful gift and delight his heart. However, judging from my mail and counseling appointments, many women do not understand how important, both physically and psychologically, the sexual relationship is to their husband. They do not seem to realize that their avoidance of sex or their lack of response will affect their entire marriage in the most negative way. To the indifferent wife I must give this caution: When there is no physical intimacy between you and your husband, whatever emotional and spiritual closeness you have had will tend to fade as well."[6]

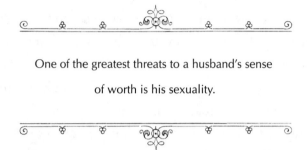

One of the greatest threats to a husband's sense
of worth is his sexuality.

No one explains the benefits of a wife's sexual responsiveness better than Kevin Leman. In his excellent book *Sheet Music,* he writes:

A sexually fulfilled husband will do anything for you. Sex is such a basic need for men that when this area is well taken care of, they feel immense appreciation and act accordingly. A sexually fulfilled man drives to work thinking, *I'm so glad I married that woman. I must be the happiest man alive!* And then heads home thinking, *What special thing can I do for my wife this evening? . . .* Instead of resenting requests to stop by the store or take a look at a leaky faucet, a sexually fulfilled man will jump with eagerness. Instead of being cold and distant when you talk to him, he's going to want to hear what you have to say.

Some wives reading this may be thinking, *I tried that, and it didn't work.* You can't just "try" this; it has to become a way of life. One good time of sex will make a man thankful—for a while. But if he's turned down the next five times, he'll think about the five rejections, not that one special night. . . .

A sexually fulfilled husband will feel good about himself. So much of who we are as men is tied into how our wives respond to us sexually. . . . [E]very healthy man wants to be his wife's hero. . . . He may not be the top dog at work, he may not have the fastest car, . . . his hair may be falling out while his gut is getting bigger, but if his honey loves him enough to occasionally put a few scratches on his back in the heat of passion, he will still feel like the king of the world. Why? Because he can please his woman.[7]

Responding to your husband's sexual advances will build his sexual confidence and make him more tender and attentive. He will become a confident lover who pleases you in mature, appropriate ways. Although a wife typically needs tenderness before sex, a husband often needs a sexual release to experience tenderness.

Although a wife typically needs tenderness before sex, a husband

often needs a sexual release to experience tenderness.

"And remember," writes Shaunti Feldhahn in her book *For Women Only,* "if you do respond physically but do it just to meet his needs without getting engaged, you're not actually meeting his needs. In fact, you might as well send him out to clip the hedges. So enjoy God's intimate gift, and make the most of it!"[8]

Husbands, allow us to offer a few insights about your wife's responsiveness. First, remember that sexual responsiveness is different for men and women. Men can be ready for sex immediately. A wife could say, "Hey, want to—" and a husband could answer yes before she even finishes the question. No arm twisting with him! He is ready to go. Why? Because men think about sex regularly, which means they need no preparation time.

Women are different. They think about sex far less frequently, possibly as little as a few times a month. Those Hollywood tales in which women are hot to go in response to a seductive look? That's all they are: Hollywood tales—written mostly by men who . . . think about sex many times a day. But when a husband suggests having sex with his wife, chances are that she was not thinking at all about sex that day. So she probably is *not* in the mood for a romp in the sack.

When a husband says, "Hey, honey, want to have sex?" this is often what happens in his wife's mind: *Hmm,* she thinks, *sex. Sex. I hadn't thought about that. Let's see, I still have to finish the dishes, Joe needs me to wash his football uniform for tomorrow, and I need to call Sally back to tell her I will bake cookies for tomorrow morning's book club meeting. Sex. Yeah, that does sound pretty good.*

By the time she is ready to tell her husband "Yes, I'd like that," often he has already read her hesitancy as a no. He's feeling rejected and starts to get impatient and frustrated. And before she can say yes, he gets ticked off.

Upset by her husband's behavior, the wife's thought is, *Well, yeah, sex does sound good . . . but not with you.* The husband blew it. He *could* have had sex, but because he failed to understand that it takes his wife longer to respond, he reacted negatively and reaped a self-fulfilling prophecy: He ain't getting any sex tonight.[9]

Second, wives need to be treated with respect and honor. No wife wants to feel that her husband sees her as a sex object or that he is using her for his sexual pleasure. Sometimes what you hope will be a turn-on may be a turn-off to her. Learn what makes your wife feel cherished and safe.

Third, remember that although you can compartmentalize, set aside unresolved issues, and still have sex, it's not that simple for your wife. Amanda sums it up well: "Sometimes when Dan wants to have sex, I'm not ready because I'm still bothered by things. If what I'm upset about involves Dan, then we need to clear the air before I can give myself to him. Even if what upsets me has nothing to do with him, it's still really difficult for me to respond. I'm trying to learn not to make Dan suffer because I have unresolved stuff in my head, but I need his patience."

Fourth, some women have trouble with sex. One woman wrote to us and said, "I'm not interested in having sex with my husband. If it were up to me, I could go the rest of my life not having sex. I love my husband, and I've prayed for God to give me an active sex drive, but it just isn't happening." A number of things could be happening in this woman's life—or in her marriage—but two possibilities are that she has been hurt by past sexual abuses or that her body's hormonal system may not be functioning normally. We treat both of those issues in later chapters. If your wife's unresponsiveness is serious, the two of you may need to dig deeper. Your wife may need to see a physician. If she has suffered sexual hurt, then you may need to consider asking a Christian counselor to help you to find healing for those hurts.

Wives, allow us to offer a few insights for you as well. First, as we said in the previous paragraph, some women have trouble with sex. Kelly told us at a conference that she is reluctant to have sex because she rarely experiences orgasm. She mentally associates sex with feelings of frustration and disappointment. She asked, "Why would I respond if I know it won't be sexually pleasing for me?" Kelly is not alone. In one study, the American Medical Association learned that 40 percent of women between the ages of 18 and 59 reported that they experience some sort of sexual dysfunction, leading them to a loss of desire to make love.[10]

If you aren't experiencing orgasm, visit a physician who can test your adrenal system to determine if your body is sufficiently producing the hormones it needs. If testing reveals no physical reason for your inability to have an orgasm, then look at stresses, medications, past history of sexual pain or hurts, or other factors that could be affecting your body. See chapter 8 for a fuller discussion of these factors. The bottom line is many women have difficulty experiencing orgasm. But don't accept that as your fate for life. Try to find some solutions that will enhance your sexual life—and your husband's as a result.

Second, if you are battling negative attitudes about sex because of your upbringing or other sources, work to balance your perspective. Jasmine told us, "My mom and grandmother pounded into my head that sex was dirty. How do I take all that training from the women in my life and still become the sexy woman I know my husband wants? As soon as I get into the mood, those messages bounce around in my head, and I get turned off before I get started." Our attitudes are shaped by many forces: peers, family, the media, and ads, to name a few. If you struggle with harmful attitudes, ask God for help. Allow the Bible to shape your attitude. Remember that God created the marriage relationship and sex—and called his creation *good*. If you need additional help balancing your attitude, talk to a trusted friend or a biblical counselor.

WHAT HAPPENS WHEN A HUSBAND'S SEX NEEDS ARE NOT MET?

In their book *The Married Guy's Guide to Great Sex,* Christian sex therapists Clifford and Joyce Penner discuss what happens when men struggle with sex: "When a sexual struggle invades your relationship, it attacks your self-esteem—and your wife's. As you feel worse about yourselves, both of you will respond with characteristic weaknesses. You may withdraw, become more aggressive, deliver put-downs, show frustration or anger, or otherwise damage your relationship. Sexual dilemmas have a way of perpetuating themselves. . . . Spouses avoid each other because they don't want to fail again. When they finally do connect, both are anxious and feel pressure to succeed. The likelihood of success lessens, and the problem grows."[11]

A few years ago a woman sent us this e-mail: "Last night, while lying in bed, my husband said, 'Is it safe to say that I don't turn you on and you have no desire to have sex with me?' I had to be totally honest and say, 'Yes, and I don't know why. I wish it weren't like this. It breaks my heart that we aren't sexually on the same page.'"

A wife needs to understand that when she makes only a halfhearted effort to have sex with her husband, he hears these messages:

- "I'd rather be doing ten other things than making love to you right now. You're just not worth my effort."
- "You don't do anything right."
- "You don't attract me the way you used to."

When a husband receives those messages—whether or not they are what his wife intends—he feels rejected and reacts in several ways.

1. He may withdraw sexually and emotionally. When a man feels disrespected and disconnected, he may not verbalize it well. Instead he may withdraw. When a wife rejects her husband's request for sex, it's not that he feels the attempt failed; he feels that *he's* a failure. A wife can say, "That's not what I'm communicating." Maybe so, but that's how it *feels* to her husband. Even when she says no for a valid reason, rejection to a man spells one thing: rejection. And when the rejection happens often enough, he will shut down.

2. He may become angry and resentful. When a man's need is unmet, he will try to fix it, control it, or change it. If he can't, before he pulls away and goes elsewhere (to solitude or to another woman), he may grow frustrated and then angry. The frustration arises from being misunderstood, disrespected, or unheard. Unresolved anger then becomes bitterness or resentment, ultimately resulting in isolation.

He may express disappointment. He may not be able to say, "I feel disappointed," but you can sense his disappointment. He may frown or pout. His anger may be passive-aggressive: not cooperating, not listening, avoiding contact, or coming home late from work with no phone call. Or his anger may come out through criticism or harsh comments.

One man wrote this sad story and sent it to us:

I have craved sexual fulfillment from my wife for thirty-four years. Sex has been a sore spot since the first week of marriage. For years I've asked and begged her for physical intimacy. Rarely has she responded. A few times when we made love, she seemed to receive pleasure from it, and a few times I felt satisfied, as if I'd rediscovered the woman I married. I've tried so hard not to need sex, and not to blame her. Hundreds of times I tried to wait until she wanted me, but she never did. Finally, about three years ago I gave up. It's the only way I've had any peace about the sad condition of our marriage.

Last weekend I took her to our favorite bed-and-breakfast place. The first morning I mentioned making love. She said, "I probably can't because of my back." I accepted that; I really wasn't surprised. But she half-heartedly participated in relieving me. The rest of the weekend I didn't ask any more. As we were leaving, she expressed concern that we hadn't made love. Then on the way home she brought it up again. I could feel myself becoming angry, and the more I thought about it, the madder I got. I wanted to say something to her, but

I knew that if I accused her of being the reason we didn't have sex, she would cry, and nothing would be done about our problem. I can't stand this anymore.

Many of a man's emotions go through the gate of anger. Fear, frustration, irritability, sadness, rejection, hurt—all are usually expressed through anger. This man, while expressing anger, was also experiencing all these other emotions. Pent-up anger eventually is manifested in isolation, resentment, bitterness, and depression. If a husband is expressing anger regarding sex, invariably this strong emotion is a secondary emotion, covering an emotion even more vulnerable.

3. He may become vulnerable to sexual temptation. Although a husband may not physically cheat on his wife, he may begin to fantasize or lust after other women. That's what happened to Greg. During their eleven-year marriage, Greg's wife, Kristi, rarely had sex with him, and when she did, she usually told him, "Let's make this quick so I can go to sleep."

"After several years of this," Greg told Gary, "I began to think that this was just my lot in life and that I would need to learn to live with it. 'I can do all things through Christ who gives me strength,' right? But it's not working out that way. My job requires that I work closely with several women, and they have expressed an interest in me. Until lately, I've never considered being unfaithful to my wife. But my wife's rejection of me (which is not the way she sees it) has led to a fantasy life, and I've found myself drawn to other women who don't think it would be so horrible to be intimate with me. I can't believe I'm having these thoughts. But I just can't shake them."

The opportunity for sexual fulfillment outside marriage is constantly available to a man. Even though a husband is personally responsible for staying faithful and maintaining sexual boundaries, a wife's behavior contributes to his vulnerability to temptation.

Even though a husband is personally responsible for staying faithful and maintaining sexual boundaries, a wife's behavior contributes to his vulnerability to temptation.

Most men are used to seeing responses to their actions. Work brings a paycheck. Running breaks a sweat. Initiation leads to a response in many areas of his life. But when a wife rejects his initiation of sex, he becomes upset—sometimes passively, other times indirectly, and maybe even overtly.

In *Making Sense of the Men in Your Life,* Kevin Leman writes, "Wife, in the twenty-first century, sexual disinterest on your part is flat out dangerous. Maybe in the Garden of Eden, where sexual images didn't abound, sexual apathy could be managed. But this isn't the Garden of Eden, and your husband isn't living in a pure world. If you want him to be faithful, the least you can do is never give him a reason to look elsewhere."[12]

As a wife, you have great influence on your husband's sex life. When you commit to fully engage with him before, during, and after sex, you help keep him fully focused on you.

QUIZ: ARE YOU CONNECTING TO YOUR HUSBAND IN THE WAY HE NEEDS?

Respond with a yes or no to the following statements:

- *I regularly tell him that he is my one and only and that when we connect intellectually, emotionally, and spiritually, sex is a grand slam.*
- *I dress provocatively—for my husband's eyes only.*
- *I am alert to times when my husband's sexual needs have built up, and then I initiate sex with him.*
- *I flirt with my husband by teasing him sexually, and then I fulfill his sexual desires.*
- *I connect to my husband's mind by discovering and affirming his thoughts, ideas, and dreams. I know what brings him passion.*
- *I am willing to have fun during sex.*
- *When I see my husband guard his eyes from provocative TV or movie scenes or women in public, I affirm his godliness and commitment to me.*
- *I love my husband completely and move beyond the top layer of emotion to help him understand what other feelings he may be experiencing.*
- *I enjoy connecting to him spiritually and reminding him that his spiritual thirst makes me want to give to him sexually.*

How did you respond to the statements in the quiz? If you answered yes to the majority of the statements, you are likely connecting to your husband's sexual needs—and others he may have. If you answered no to the majority, then learn to affirm the positive areas, be teachable on the ones you didn't affirm, and ask God to give you eyes and an open heart for change.

How to Meet Your Husband's Sex Needs

The previous paragraphs are reminders of what can happen when a husband's needs are not met. We encourage you to invest in your husband. Love him. Meet his needs—for his sake and for the sake of your marriage. How can you do that? Pick a few of the following suggestions, and begin the process of meeting your husband's sex needs.

1. Realize sex plays a major role in helping men process life. Sex has the miraculous ability to clear a man's mind, helping him solve problems. Women often resolve problems by talking things out; men often solve problems when they have sex with their wives.

2. Say yes as often as possible. The fastest connection charger is to say yes to sex. Basically, if a wife gets only one thing from this chapter, it needs to be the importance of saying yes. If she wants to connect with her husband, the best way to do that is through sex.

3. If you must say no, don't say it right away. When your husband wants to be involved sexually with you, don't immediately close the door. Recognize it as a real need and consider that your positive response is one way you can love and serve your husband. Again, remember the apostle Paul's words: "Love is patient and kind. . . . It does not demand its own way."[13] Then, if you must say no, be prepared to do two things: Give an honest reason for the delay, and then suggest a time when you might be more ready to respond to his needs.

4. Decide to enjoy sex. Sex actually starts in the mind. You can choose to enjoy sex, or you can choose not to enjoy sex. Your decision becomes a trajectory for your relationship—inside and outside the bedroom. In a majority of couples we talk to, we find that women really do enjoy sex when they start out by choosing to enjoy it.

5. Help your spouse know how to please you. If your husband does not know how to please you, teach him. Men are not mind readers—especially in bed. The great myth is that men automatically know how to be great lovers. Where did this myth come from? Where do we think men learn these great secrets to passion? The junior high locker room? Not exactly the pinnacle of great knowledge. The movies? Again, not real life. Your husband needs to know what gives you pleasure. When you are making love, place your hand over his and lead him. Whisper in his ear what you would really like him to do. There is nothing embarrassing or shameful about that kind of communication.

6. Get over shyness. God designed us to be sexual, to be vulnerable. Wives, start to voice your needs. When you become more specific about what you desire in the bedroom, both of you will benefit. Trust us, a husband will not respond in disgust or outrage. Husbands, make sure that you do not misuse that trust. What you and your wife do is not something to share with your buddies. What happens in the bedroom is private.

7. Realize your husband's emotions may not work like yours. A woman easily shifts from one emotion to another. For instance, if her husband doesn't talk to her much, she may think, *What did I do wrong this time? Is he sick of me? Do I make him do too much around the house? Does he think I'm fat and old? Maybe there's someone at the office he finds more interesting and attractive.*

Women can go from point A to point Z in a matter of sixty seconds. Meanwhile, he's thinking, *I'm really tired. I can't wait to watch that action movie tonight.* Many men don't think beyond the first emotion unless there's a problem to be solved. They don't usually overanalyze or go down the list of cause-and-effect. Wives will make progress in their marriages when they realize this truth.

8. Take the 10 percent challenge. Wives, what would happen if you responded sexually to your husband 10 percent more than you do now? When can you start applying this challenge? The next time your husband says something that sounds like this: "I was thinking, maybe we could hire a babysitter Saturday night and spend some time alone." "I feel like turning in early tonight. Could we put the kids to bed now?" "We haven't made love for a few weeks. Can we have some private time?"

Many women ask us, "Am I meeting his need if I respond a lot but not every time?" Yes, but really, that's the wrong question. The number is not important. What matters is the *nature* of the response and the connection that happens when you and your husband work toward anticipation and sexual satisfaction. Even a small shift in your responsiveness can bring your husband much joy and improve your marriage.

9. Create a game plan. It may help to set up a game plan so that your husband will not take your hesitancy personally. The game plan can include the following aspects:

- *If you must say no, be clear about the reason.* If Anita is not sexually responsive to her husband's advances, she'll tell him why. It may be fatigue, fear the kids will overhear, or unresolved conflict. Instead of withdrawing, she communicates and graciously tells Tim what she is feeling. When he understands what she sees as obstacles, he is better able to work toward resolving the issue. Sometimes they are unable to settle a problem, and they agree to hold off on trying to connect sexually. But then they promise to try again in the next day or two.

- *Know what to expect.* When a wife is not able to respond, one of the best things she can do is to let her husband know when he can expect to have sex, whether it is later that night or the next day. That usually resolves the situation much better than saying, "I don't feel like it" and going to sleep. Talk together about how many times a week you would like to have sex so that both of you know what the expectations are. Some of you may feel awkward about planning ahead for sex, as if putting it on the calendar makes it feel forced. Yet planning ahead works for many couples, taking the guesswork and conflict out of the situation and giving the couple rhythm and anticipation. If a husband knows he and his wife will have sex once per week (or three times a week or more), he can start enhancing the connection that leads to an enthusiastic response from his wife.

- *Follow up on a promise for sex.* If you must say no, make sure that your no is "not right now, but soon." We received this e-mail message from Todd: "My wife and I are not intimate on a regular basis (once every month). We have been married almost eighteen years. I am honestly trying to meet her needs, but I have basically given up on chasing her to make love. Half the time she feels I am hounding her, and the other half she says 'yes, but later.' That would be great, if 'later' ever came."

This is so important. Wives, follow through on your "later." We know that sometimes "later" has to be changed too. But a healthy marriage is based on trust; your spouse should be able to trust that you will follow through on what you say. When "later" never comes, pretty soon your spouse will doubt your word—not only in the area of sex but in other areas as well.

- *Know each other's needs and sexual rhythms, and show empathy.* "If I need to say no to Terry," Robin explained, "I'd never just say no and leave it up to his imagination to guess why—especially because I know that when he's disappointed, he always thinks the worst. Then I take his emotional pulse. I may ask him, 'Is this a time when you really need it, no matter what?' If his answer is yes (I can trust him to be honest with me), then I put aside my own needs and enjoy meeting his. I never engage in sex if I would be bitter or angry during or afterward. Or I will consider the last time we had sex; if more than two days have passed since then, I take his desire seriously. Or I will ask myself if our lovemaking would help him think clearer the next day or reduce his stress or help him fight the battle of purity better. Or I may ask him, 'Is this just a bonus time?' If it is and if I can't change my attitude, then we plan to have sex another time."

CHAPTER 6

A Wife's Other Sex Needs

In the previous two chapters we discussed the top three sex needs for both men and women. For all the differences men and women have, our survey suggests that husbands and wives essentially want the same things in their sex lives: relationship, intimacy, and fulfillment. The differences arise from the ways we pursue those needs: men through the physical act, women through emotional connection. In the next two chapters, we'll look at the final top sex needs of men and women. You may be interested to see that these needs are interconnected as well.

The women in our survey indicated that their other two sex needs are spiritual intimacy and romance. How are these two needs connected? Both spiritual intimacy and romance are things you do outside the bedroom and that you do for and with your spouse. The result when both needs are fulfilled is an enhanced sex life.

SPIRITUAL INTIMACY

It was finally out. Through tears of frustration, Sharla told her husband, Jeremy, that she was miserable.

"What?" Jeremy asked her. "How can you be miserable? You have everything you could possibly need. You don't have to work, I have a sizable income, we live in a great place, we take wonderful vacations, I'm faithful to you. What more do you want?"

"I constantly ask you to go to church with me, to pray with me, but you refuse."

"That's what this is about?" he asked, incredulous. "You're miserable in our marriage because I don't do the church thing? That's just not me, Sharla. And anyway, I go with you sometimes."

"But I have to beg you."

"I just don't feel comfortable there. Why can't we just agree we have separate interests and leave it at that?"

A husband often does all he can to take care of his wife by providing for her, but sometimes he doesn't tend her soul, her spirit, her innermost beliefs and passions. His spiritually starved wife would often trade all the vacations in the world for a little spiritual intimacy from her husband.

A husband often does all he can to take care of his wife by providing for her, but sometimes he doesn't tend her soul, her spirit, her innermost beliefs and passions.

How is tending to your wife's spiritual side a sexual need? Women all over the country tell us the same thing: "When my husband takes the lead spiritually, by praying, reading his Bible, or going to church, I am drawn to him on a deep level. It makes me feel so secure that I am eager to give myself fully to him."

Women are so serious about spiritual intimacy with their husbands that 58 percent ranked it as a top sex need. If you think it's just our survey respondents who feel spiritual things affect what goes on in the bedroom, take a look at a survey conducted by the National Marriage Project, located at Rutgers University. Prominent family experts David Popenoe and Barbara Dafoe Whitehead reexamined the institution of marriage in America. In 2001, Gallup collected the data for the National Marriage Project study, which included interviews from 1,003 adults who ranged in age from twenty to twenty-nine. The results indicate that emotional and *spiritual* connection rank far above other needs, including financial stability, in forming a romantic partnership. Nearly 81 percent of the women interviewed reported that it is more important to have a husband who can communicate about his deepest feelings than it is to have a husband who earns a good living. An overwhelming majority (94 percent) believe that a spouse should be a soul mate first and foremost.[1]

What does that information tell us? Women want men who can connect to the deepest part of them—the spiritual part.

In *Making Love Last Forever*, Gary Smalley writes about finding the power to keep loving: "Why is the spiritual journey so important? Marriage researchers are finding a correlation between one's spiritual journey and one's satisfaction in marriage. Howard Markman, Scott Stanley, and Susan Blumberg report that religion has a favorable impact on marriage. They write that religious couples 'are less likely to divorce . . . show somewhat higher levels of satisfaction . . . lower levels of conflict about common issues . . . and higher levels of commitment.'"[2] Similarly, marriage expert Nick Stinnett found that one characteristic common to most happy marriages and families was an active, shared faith in God.[3]

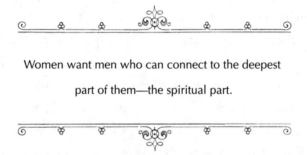

Women want men who can connect to the deepest
part of them—the spiritual part.

If you want to release deep passion in your wife, then get serious about connecting with her spiritually.

WHAT IS SPIRITUAL INTIMACY?

You will experience deep spiritual intimacy when you have a mutual, heartfelt desire to be close to God, when you seek God's direction for your marriage—even for your sex life. Spiritual intimacy means that in the midst of conflict, you honor and respect each other. You don't put each other down in an attempt to win; you think about how God would want you to act in the situation. You become united together through prayer. You unite under biblical principles for your lives and marriage. You actively invite God into every aspect of your marriage, including sex.

A wife deeply desires to pursue God *with* her husband. She wants to have spiritual conversations, to read the Bible together, and to pray together. A wife is attracted to a husband when he provides spiritual leadership.

Your wife needs you to be her "soul protector."

God designed the husband to be the spiritual leader in the marriage. And your wife really wants to see you succeed in that. When you spiritually lead your wife, she feels encouraged to trust you more. When a husband and wife build their marriage on the foundational commitment to pursue God above all, they are able to share fears, anxieties, joys, and dreams. They are free to experience transparent honesty, knowing that they love each other unconditionally and that neither will ever walk away.

HOW TO MEET YOUR WIFE'S NEED FOR SPIRITUAL INTIMACY

Pick a few of the following suggestions, and begin the process of meeting your wife's need for spiritual intimacy.

1. Ask your wife what she needs. The best way to start meeting your wife's need is to ask her how she would like you to build spiritual intimacy with her. Don't let her give general answers. Probe exactly what she means. If she says, "I want you to be the spiritual leader in our marriage," ask her what that looks like to her on a daily, practical level. Then begin to follow her requests.

2. Be honest about your awkward feelings. In the *Reader's Digest* article "How Honest Are Couples, Really?" the author reported the results of a poll showing that men wish they could talk about deeper matters than sports or money—but they don't know how. Nearly a third of the men wished they could talk openly with their wives about spiritual matters. Marriage researcher John Gottman commented on this finding: "That really impressed me. It underscores the meaning of how we live, what we value. It's hard for men to talk about that."[4]

In a similar Canadian study, 42 percent of both husbands and wives wished they could talk openly with their spouses about spiritual matters. "This reinforces the notion that a lot of people today feel an emptiness with regard to spirituality and values and would like to talk to their partner about that," says Sue Johnson, executive director of the Ottawa Couple and Family Institute.[5]

If you are uncomfortable talking about spiritual things, start slowly. One great way to start is for each of you to share the history of your spiritual life. Use the following questions to discover more about your partner's faith:

- What did your parents believe about God, Jesus, church, prayer, and the Bible?
- How and where did you first learn about God, Jesus, and the Holy Spirit? At what age?
- What questions about faith did you have as a child and teenager? Who gave you the answers?

- Did you memorize any Bible verses as a child? Which of those verses do you remember now?
- As a child, if you could have asked God any questions, what would they have been?
- If you could ask God any questions now, what would they be?
- When you were a child, did anyone you looked up to as a Christian disappoint you? If so, how has that influenced you as an adult?
- How have difficult times affected your faith?
- What has been the greatest spiritual experience of your life?

4. Pray *for* your wife. More than anything else—more than flowers, candy, candlelit dinners, or gifts—your wife needs you to be her "soul protector." Pray for her throughout the day. Pray for her struggles and her dreams. Ask God to show you ways to meet her needs.

5. Pray *with* your wife. Praying together is probably the strongest knot that binds a couple. Praying together may feel uncomfortable in the beginning, so use these tips to minimize self-consciousness and make you aware of God's presence in your life.

- Set aside time to pray together. It could be first thing in the morning or any other time of the day that works for you. If doing it daily seems like a stretch, pray together once a week, maybe on Sunday evening. If you are comfortable, pray together while taking a walk or driving in the car.

- Share prayer requests regularly. Informing each other of your needs is an important way to open your hearts to each other and to know where to start in meeting each other's needs.
- Talk about how God has answered your prayers in the past.
- Start with a few minutes of silent prayer.
- When you are with your wife, put your arms around her and pray, "I ask God to bless you. I take your needs and present them to God for his direction. I am so grateful that you are my wife."
- Pray out loud together for each other, for your marriage, and for your family.
- Pray the Bible together. Try reading the psalms as prayers.
- Buy a book of prayers, and pray them together.
- Read together our thirty-day devotional, *Renewing Your Love*, which offers daily topics to strengthen your marriage, questions to help you share with each other, and prayers to connect you spiritually.

6. Encourage your wife spiritually. To get started, complete these four statements together:

- You could help me grow in my faith by . . .
- I feel most comfortable praying with you when we . . .
- We could grow together in our faith if we . . .
- We could serve God together by . . . [6]

7. Become a spiritual sounding board. Tune in and listen to your wife. If she has a greater need to talk about spiritual things than you do, don't be put off. Listen. Ask questions. Share your insights with her.

8. Focus on your wife's spiritual strengths. When you see her make a difficult decision based on her convictions, affirm and encourage her. When you are drawn to God because of her, let her know.

9. Practice forgiveness. When you and your wife have an argument or when she has hurt or frustrated you in some way, know that any unresolved offense can block all kinds of intimacy—emotional, physical, and spiritual. When you sense a wall between you and your spouse, something is wrong. Take responsibility for your wrongs. Ask for forgiveness. And when your wife does the same, choose to forgive her. (If you need help in this area, we suggest our book *Healing the Hurt in Your Marriage*, a detailed look at how to resolve conflict in a marriage.)

ROMANCE

The sex need that rated the fifth highest among women in our survey was romance. Nearly 53 percent of the women placed romance as a top sex need. We suspect that many of you men are thinking, *Okay. Of all of my wife's sex needs, this is the one I know the most about. This is where I'm the expert. I'm the love doctor.*

Men, we hate to break this to you, but most women do not equate romance with sex. Several years ago we conducted a survey about how husbands and wives defined *romance,* and we found that men and women are quite different in this area. Of the husbands we surveyed, 50 percent said the most romantic thing their wife ever did for them involved sex, 25 percent said it involved food, and 25 percent said it involved doing something together. Of the women we surveyed, *not one of them* directly mentioned sex in their understanding of romance; most of them felt that romance resulted from spending quality time together.

A wife feels romanced when her husband does anything that shows he cares for her and thinks about her: special phone calls or notes, surprises, something out of the ordinary on an ordinary day. She feels romanced when her husband talks with her without distractions, when he holds her hand and kisses her every morning.

Romance is the bridge between love and sex, so when a wife's need for romance is not met, she struggles to move toward sex. She views her husband more as preoccupied and distant than as her lover. Will she still agree to have sex? Probably. But it's not as exciting or enjoyable for her as it could be.

Romance is the bridge between love and sex.

Gregory Godek, writer, speaker, husband, and incurable romantic, shares his passion for romance in his book *1001 Ways to Be Romantic*. He says, "Romance creates a context within which sexuality can be given more meaning. Romance focuses sexuality toward a loving purpose: The growth of intimacy. Without romance, sex is just seduction. Without romance, sex can turn into an empty habit or dull duty. With romance, sex becomes connected to love. With romance, sex becomes about giving, not merely taking."[7]

Many things can deter romance: misunderstandings, the distractions of home, work, kids, and life. But without frequent doses of romance, a sexual relationship will get boring and shrivel up. Romance is a must if you want your sexual intimacy to deepen.

Several years ago Dr. Phil surveyed 37,000 people and learned a lot about the importance of romance.

> Not surprisingly, romance is central to our definition of love: Ninety-four percent respond that giving flowers, holding hands, or taking your partner for a night out are hallmarks of love (only 6 percent say those are signs of guilt or duty). Yet almost two-thirds also characterize mundane chores such as taking out the trash, bathing the kids, or doing the dishes as acts of love. What these actions say to your mate is, *I want your life to be better, and I'll make personal sacrifices to ensure that.* Our respondents don't appear to be materialistic or superficial. . . . Money isn't a factor, and appearance doesn't seem to matter, either—82 percent wouldn't love their partners any less if he or she gained 100 pounds. *Honesty, listening, giving, respect,* and *tenderness* were words that those polled most clearly associate with love. . . . The core element of true love is that you feel like you belong; romantics call it having a soul mate.[8]

So what is romance? Love is a *feeling;* romance is love in *action.* Romance is something you do to express the love that you feel. How do you do that? The key is to know your wife. One wife commented that her husband thinks buying a card is a waste of three dollars, so she doesn't buy him cards. But he gives her cards because he knows it gives her delight. Some women think of romance as a candlelit dinner at home, while others need to leave home for romance. Some women are bothered if their husbands spend money they don't have, so they prefer a picnic at a park rather than a fancy meal. Romance must be tailored to your wife's unique preferences.

Love is a *feeling;* romance is love in *action.*

One thing you can do is ask yourself this question: When I was dating my wife and trying to win her heart, what really got her attention? Men tend to stop thinking about those things once they get married. They feel that once they've won the girl, the work is done. From there on out, it's easy sailing. But that simply isn't true. A husband needs to realize that life's responsibilities have a way of wearing down his wife. She needs him to romance her all over again.

When men hear the word *romance,* they often become intimidated. Two images pop into their heads: a dollar sign (money) and a clock ticking (time). They imagine they'll have to spend a week thinking of what to do, a week planning the special event, and a week earning the money to pay for it! Some guys immediately shove the idea of romance off, thinking, *That sappy, mushy stuff isn't for me.*

But the *real* reason many men feel intimidated by romance is because they fear rejection. Perhaps a man has asked his wife several times to reserve two Saturday nights a month as date nights, but every time she has an excuse: she's tired, the kids need her, the house is a mess. Or a husband might give up romancing his wife because he's afraid she won't like his romance ideas. But allowing fear to have the upper hand will harm their desire for sexual intimacy. The passion will drain from the marriage, and apathy or resentment will grow.

What gets in the way of romance? When we surveyed couples about their ideas on romance, we asked them to tell us their biggest obstacle to romance. These are some of their responses:

- Busyness and fatigue
- Distractions—work, church, unresolved conflict
- Financial stress
- Disappointments—"I was thinking of dinner at a low-light, quiet restaurant; he was thinking of the pizza buffet at Village Pub."
- Unwilling hearts
- Lack of creativity
- Chores left to do
- Indifference

How to Meet Your Wife's Need for Romance

Husbands, we have good news. According to our survey, romancing your wife often means doing simple things that don't require much time or money. One wife said, "It's the little things that make me realize how much he cares for me."

Pick a few of the following suggestions, and begin the process of meeting your wife's need for romance.

1. Learn your wife's love needs. What makes your wife feel cherished and deeply loved? Study her. Ask her what romance means to her and how you can meet that need. Then really listen to her answers.

2. Be tender. An important element of romance is tenderness. Hold her hand and caress it. Touch her face. Tenderly play with her hair. Remind her why you fell in love with her.

3. Show your wife that you care. Pay attention to what your wife likes. For instance, Alice likes to dress up when she and her husband go out, but her husband doesn't. It means a lot to her when he takes a shower, smells good, and puts on nice clothes when they go out to eat.

Jennifer told us this story about how her husband made the effort to let her know he cared. "I used to travel a lot for work, and one night my flight home was cancelled. I knew the delay would threaten a deadline on an important project at work. I called my husband from the airport, and as soon as I heard his voice, I was in tears. I missed being home. I drove back to my hotel, and twenty minutes later I heard a knock on my door. A hotel staff member brought me my favorite ice cream—at my husband's request."

4. Remember days that are important to your wife. Fill your calendar or PDA with reminders for your wife's birthday, significant anniversaries she would want to celebrate, Valentine's Day, and any other days that are important to her. Then celebrate those days with a card, gift, flowers, a getaway—whatever is meaningful to your wife. If you're not sure what she likes, ask her.

5. Surprise her. Women love to be surprised. You can do that in so many simple ways. Write a love message on a Post-it note, and put it on your bathroom mirror. Make her breakfast some morning. Give her a card for no other reason than to say "I was thinking about you." Take home a treat she likes. Send her flowers at home or work. Give your wife an at-home spa experience. Run a hot bath with some of your wife's favorite fragrance, place lit candles all around the bathroom, and tell her to relax for as long as she wants. Plan a date night, but don't let your wife know where you are going. Ask her to be ready at a certain time, and let her know what kind of dress would be appropriate for the occasion. Then enjoy your night out together.

6. Occasionally make a splash. Judie told us this story. "After thirty years of marriage, we felt like we had done it all: weekends away, dinners and movies, sports games of all kinds, picnics, and walks. And being a woman over fifty, I wasn't so excited to get into the same dress and go out for dinner. But my husband managed to do something to spin my head around! A week before our date, he told me, 'You are my Cinderella, and I want you to feel like it.' When I got home from work one night, on the bed was my Cinderella dress—an outfit he picked out and bought for me. He laid it on the bed as if there were a person in it! It was beautiful—my size and my favorite color. In our bedroom he had set a small table on which he placed some exquisite hors d'oeuvres he'd bought from my favorite bakery. He put some of our childhood photos on the table, and in the center he had placed a flower. After we ate the food, he said, 'I want you to experience the magic of Cinderella, so we're going to the Cinderella play.' I really enjoyed the play, but the night wasn't over yet. My husband announced that we were going to the Princess Castle and took me to my favorite restaurant. Not only did he make me feel young and beautiful, but he had thought through the outfit, the hors d'oeuvres, our photos, the play tickets, and my favorite restaurant. It's so awesome to be loved like that!" Most of us can't afford that kind of splash very often, but once in a while it's good to make a memory.

7. **Share secret "special somethings."** "Romance is something he does just for me—not for anyone else," said Nikki. "For instance, he always taps out 'I love you' on my arm or shoulder when we're in a crowd and can't verbally say it. It reminds me that he's thinking of me and loves me." Another woman said, "When we're in public or as I'm driving away from the house, my husband will hold up three fingers, which means 'I love you.'" Create a secret code that only you and your wife share.

8. **Get away.** As family responsibilities and challenges mount, husbands and wives lose track of each other's needs. Sometimes it takes getting away from the pressures at home to get to know your spouse again. Plan a night to be together. Go for a long drive in the country, and take roads you've never taken before. Enjoy the adventure. Leave town—without the kids! Take mini-vacations.

9. **Shake things up a little.** Instead of doing the normal dinner-and-a-movie date, go see a foreign film or some quirky independent film. Instead of eating a meal on the deck, throw a blanket in the backyard and eat PB and J sandwiches. Lie outside on a blanket and count the stars, then for each star, say something you adore about your wife.

10. If you think it, do it. In his article "Strategic Romance," Jim Mueller writes, "If you have a romantic thought during the day, take action! Pick up the phone and make the dinner reservation; stop by the [card store] and pick up the card; call your wife and tell her 'I love you.' I'm on a first name basis with my florist. All I need to do is pick up the phone and put the order on my account—it doesn't get easier than that."[9]

A ROMANCE CHECKLIST
Need some more ideas for romance? Check out Greg Godek's Romance Checklist.[10]

Daily:
Compliment your partner.
Spend twenty minutes of uninterrupted time together.
Check in with each other during the day.
Perform one small and unexpected gesture.
Say "I love you" at least three times.
Thank your partner for something.
Look for romantic concepts in the newspaper.
Take an extra minute when kissing good-bye.

Weekly:
Bring home one small, unexpected present.
Share some form of physical intimacy.
Share an entire afternoon or evening together.
Share two insights you gained this week.
Write at least one little love note.
Mail something to your partner.
Make love!
Plan something special for the upcoming weekend.

Monthly:

Plan one romantic surprise.

Restock your stash of greeting cards.

Go out to dinner once or twice.

Rent at least two romantic movies.

Make love several times!

Make plans for a three-day romantic weekend sometime in the next three months.

Plan one romantic event with a seasonal theme.

Yearly:

Make a resolution to be more creative with romance.

Make plans for your next anniversary.

Think of an unusual way to celebrate your partner's birthday.

Review your plans for your next vacation.

Create a special "romance" category in your household budget.

Make plans for Valentine's Day well in advance!

CHAPTER 7

A Husband's Other Sex Needs

The final two sex needs that our male survey respondents listed are tied to a husband's sense of worth. A man has a strong need for his wife to initiate sex and to affirm him.

INITIATION

Mindy knew her husband, Eric, was having a rough week at work. An attorney in their small town, he'd been hired to represent a major client in a fraud case and was putting in long hours.

One evening when he arrived home, Mindy made him a cup of hot chocolate. Then she sat in front of him, slowly removed his shoes, and began to massage his feet.

"That feels good," Eric said, closing his eyes.

"I know something else that will make you feel good," Mindy said.

He opened one eye and looked at her. She raised her eyebrows and slowly moved his foot to rest between her breasts.

"I think I could be interested," he said, putting down his hot chocolate.

Mindy stood, took Eric's hand, and led him to the bedroom.

How did that make Eric feel? "I can't tell you how much my

wife's gesture meant to me. When she initiated having sex, it was as if she were screaming to me, 'I love you so much. I understand the pressure you've been under. I want to give you the gift of sex. I know how much that will please you and give you release. Let's go enjoy each other's bodies.' Whew. What guy wouldn't feel like a king after having his wife do that? Oh, and by the way, the sex was *great!*"

In an earlier chapter, when we discussed a husband's need for his wife to respond, we said that her resistance to his sexual advances affects his confidence and his view of himself. If a wife's *responsiveness* strengthens her husband's self-esteem, think about what her *initiating sex* will say to him. The men who responded to our survey thought about what it would say. Nearly 61 percent of them ranked a wife's initiation as a top sexual need.

Men enjoy spontaneity. That statement is so important for wives to understand that it bears repeating: Men love spontaneity. A husband needs his wife to initiate so he knows he's not the only one who cares about their sex life. When she initiates sex, he realizes that she cares about his needs, loves him, and thinks about him. Her initiation allows him to take a break from initiating—and the fear of her lack of response—and enjoy a spontaneous sexual encounter. A wife's initiation relieves him of the pressure of starting the process of sexual intimacy.

Men love spontaneity.

When a wife tells her husband how much she admires him or cares for him, his self-esteem is bolstered. But when she pursues him sexually, he feels on top of the world. He says to himself, *She wants me. She wants me for a lover.* He wants to shout to the world: "She still finds me attractive!"

And isn't that what you want in your marriage—a husband who is joyful, deeply satisfied, protected, and completed? Fulfill your husband's fantasy: to be desired and pursued by *you*. He doesn't want some seductress on late-night TV. He wants you—his bride.

Fulfill your husband's fantasy: to be desired and pursued by *you*.

Kevin Leman writes, "It is very emotionally fulfilling for a man to have a wife who is interested in him sexually. A man is external. If you want a man to feel wanted and needed, words won't cut it; you need to pursue him sexually."[1]

At a recent conference Suzanne told us, "If initiation is important to Greg, then I've been blind to this area in our marriage. I enjoy sex. I like to respond to him. A couple of times when we were alone at a business convention, I initiated sex, and it blew his socks off. He walked around with a twinkle in his eye that reminded me of our first year of marriage. But I thought it was a 'vacation thing.' Now I realize that I'm sending him the message that sex is important to me only if he wants it, not if I want *him*.

I'm starting to see that he would really be honored if I set the stage for sex by flirting and drawing him in."

Of all the sex needs, initiation seems to be the most difficult for many wives to practice. As we discussed in a previous chapter, most women don't regularly think about sex, so it doesn't occur to them to initiate something that isn't on their minds. But when women *do* think about sex, many figure that being responsive is good enough. In fact, some women think initiation is more a luxury than a necessary part of marriage. Well, they're wrong.

How to Meet Your Husband's Need for Initiation

Wives, be willing to step out of your comfort zone and become a sexual initiator in your marriage. Here are some ideas to get you started in meeting your husband's need for initiation.

1. Remember your husband is a sexual being. Honor your husband by taking seriously his need for sex with you. Consider it a joy and privilege to be the one God has chosen to satisfy those needs.

2. View yourself as a sexual being. "I consider myself a loving person. I love to cuddle, listen, and spend time with my husband," says Dana. "I even love romance. But I don't consider myself a sexual person. It takes effort to make me feel sexy; it doesn't come naturally." Although some women are more aware of their sexuality than others, most women do not often think on a sexual level. But when we ask women, "When you are rested, when your husband has connected to you emotionally and spiritually and you feel safe, do you feel sexy?" most women respond yes.

3. Refuse to buy into myths about sex. Women often believe that they must be in the mood to initiate sex. Here is how Clifford and Joyce Penner respond to that myth: "In real life, the more preparation, anticipation, talking, guiding and scheduling you put into your sexual times with each other, the better they likely will be. If you wait for some mysterious erotic energy to grab you before you have sex, you may not be having sex very often."[2]

4. Keep sex vibrant in your marriage. Many women think there's nothing they can do to increase or maintain their sexual desire—it just comes and goes. But remember something we've said elsewhere in this book: Sex begins in the mind. Start thinking about sex. Plan for it. Mark it on your private calendar. Initiate sex with your husband at least a couple of times each month. Save energy for sex. Pray about it, asking God to give you a desire to initiate with your husband.

The bonus of initiating is that it's on your timetable. When you initiate, you can ramp up by mentally and emotionally preparing yourself—and adjusting your to-do list accordingly. Create a "code" with your husband to let him know you're thinking about sex with him. For example, call or e-mail your husband during the day to say, "Tonight is our date night at 9:00." Your husband knows that "date night" means you want to have sex with him, and 9:00 is his time with you, no matter what.

Then prepare in ways that make sense to you. Get some ideas from these tips adapted from a list by sex therapist Douglas Rosenau:

- Budget a certain amount of money for your sex life, and spend it on lingerie, new sheets, and nights or weekends away together.

- Every now and then wear a sexy piece of lingerie all day and allow its unusual feel to remind you of sex.
- At least once a month plan a sexual surprise in which you try to arouse your husband.
- Regardless of fatigue or low interest, initiate sex at least once a week.
- Have fun with your husband's visual arousal, and let him see your nude body at unusual times just to enjoy his reactions.
- Take a bubble bath at the end of a tiring day. It's a great aphrodisiac and tunes you in to your body.
- Allow yourself to enjoy sexual images of you and your husband. Then, within boundaries you both have agreed on, make the fantasies come true later that day.
- Use a special perfume that you have associated with making love, and wear it on the evening or the day you anticipate sexual activity.[3]

5. Pay attention to your body's sexual responses. Ask God to help you recognize sexual thoughts and desires more. Even a flicker can be a great jumping-off point. Take advantage of your increased sexual urge during your hormonal cycle. A study published in *Human Reproduction* states: "Researchers speculate that a woman's libido may rise during ovulation or that her sexual attractiveness to partners may increase. It could also be that intercourse accelerates ovulation."[4]

6. Become more adventuresome. One of the biggest reasons women don't initiate is because they are nervous and afraid. Their fears say, *I don't know what I'm doing. It will be awkward* *and embarrassing. He'll laugh at me and reject me. He does it better; it's not natural for me.* Women who aren't sexually adventurous like to stick with what works. But practice will make it more natural and less awkward. Stepping out on a limb to please your husband will demonstrate your love for him. Even if it's awkward for you at first, your husband will feel honored and loved if you make the effort.

7. **Ask your husband for advice.** Outside of the bedroom, in the calm light of day, ask your husband for some specific things you can do to initiate sex with him. A husband dreams about his wife's approaching him for sex, desiring him. Ask him what his ideal sexual experience would be—and how you would initiate it. Most men have fantasies of how their wives would initiate sex. Ask your husband what he's always dreamed you would do to start making love to him. Marriage counselors David and Claudia Arp have a great idea called "Here's What I Would Like!"[5] Have your husband make a list of what he would like you to do to initiate sex. Then categorize the items on his list, using the following rating system:

- It would be my pleasure!
- I'm hesitant about this one.
- I'm not at all comfortable doing that.

This will help you communicate with your husband about what you are willing or comfortable to do to initiate sex with him—but always stay open to working toward your husband's dream (if it's appropriate).

8. **Practice.** What's the old cliché? If at first you don't succeed, try, try again. Your husband is not going to laugh at you or

reject you for breaking out of the routine to spice up your love life. Hardly. He'll most likely cheer you on. (He might even offer to work overtime just to give you some extra money to buy what you need for times of initiation.)

Sex therapists say that the more a couple have sex, the more they enjoy it. The more they enjoy it, the more they do it. Part of getting it right is enjoying sex along the way. Have fun! It's an adventure. Take the risk.

AFFIRMATION

"I don't understand why Josh is so withdrawn," Lila told Gary during a counseling session. During the entire session, she had nothing good to say about her husband. Josh slumped in his chair, staring down at his hands in his lap. In his wife's view he was unable to do anything right. Lila complained, "I honestly don't get what his problem is."

"How's your sex life?" Gary asked her.

"What sex life? I've never had an orgasm with him. He just doesn't turn me on. He's not that good in the sex department. I thought all men were supposed to know what they're doing." She laughed bitterly. "Josh sure doesn't," she said, crossing her arms and glaring at him.

"I'm beginning to see the picture," Gary said.

A smirk crossed Lila's face, as if she expected Gary to agree with her assessment of her husband's incompetence.

"Lila, when was the last time you said something nice to Josh?" Gary asked.

"What?" She looked a bit shocked.

"When was the last time you affirmed him?"

"What difference does that make?"

"It makes a lot of difference, Lila," Gary told her. "As a wife you wield a tremendous amount of power over Josh and your marriage. How you choose to handle that power will determine the strength and enjoyment of your relationship."

Every time Lila makes a derogatory comment about Josh's sexuality, it is as if she takes an ice pick to his soul. Once a proud, efficient, loving, fun man, Josh has been worn down by his wife's continual harping. Her behavior has caused him to doubt his self-worth, to withdraw, to become bitter toward her, and to stop meeting her needs altogether. His doubts about his worth and his sexual ability could begin to affect his work, his other relationships, his spiritual life, his faith.

Granted, Lila and Josh's situation seems a bit extreme, but we have heard countless conversations in which husbands and wives had nothing good to say about each other. We can only assume that if they were not verbally affirming in public, they were also not affirming inside the bedroom.

Most wives may not realize how much power their words and attitudes carry: Words can tear down their husbands or build them up. If a wife wants her husband to be all God created him to be, she needs to affirm him in every way possible.

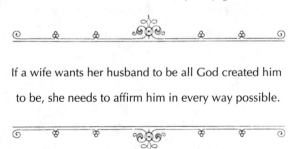

If a wife wants her husband to be all God created him

to be, she needs to affirm him in every way possible.

Affirmation is so important to a husband that 55 percent of the men who responded to our survey rated it as a top sex need. What Lila and many wives responding like her do not understand is that a man's self-esteem is often fragile—especially in the area of sex. He needs his wife—more than anyone else—to affirm his masculinity. If his wife doesn't do it, who will? Anyone can affirm his job skills or intellect or sports ability. But only a wife can get to the most sensitive, deep, vulnerable, intimate part of a man. Only his wife can affirm him sexually.

If a man finds that no one at his workplace appreciates his skill, he may look for another job in which people value what he has to offer. If no one at church appreciates his spiritual gifts, he may look for another place where they will value his contribution. Similarly, if his wife doesn't encourage, appreciate, and affirm her husband—especially his sexuality—he may look for someone else who will. A wife *alone* has the ability to make or break her husband in the vulnerable area of sexual ability. A wife is the one person who gets close enough to her husband to build or destroy him.

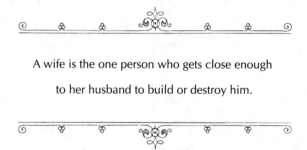

A wife is the one person who gets close enough
to her husband to build or destroy him.

The woman in the Old Testament book of Song of Songs understood the importance of affirmation. Throughout the dialogue, she boasts of her beloved's ability as a lover. Look at this passage as an example: "How handsome you are, my lover! Oh, how charming! . . . Like an apple tree among the trees of the forest is my lover among the young men. I delight to sit in his shade, and his fruit is sweet to my taste."[6] Maybe you don't feel comfortable using those words, but no husband will resist a woman who tells him, "You are an incredible lover. You turn me on. You satisfy me. I bet no other woman has a husband who satisfies her the way you satisfy me."

Without hearing those kinds of affirming words, a husband can become insecure. Or worse, hearing negative words can cripple him. Troy told us, "My wife doesn't like making love to me."

"Why not?" we asked.

He paused for a moment, looking as if he were trying to decide whether or not to state the real reason. Finally he said, "She doesn't like my sperm. She thinks sex is too messy. So she makes disgusted grunts when I have an orgasm, then makes a big production over having to clean up."

Troy's wife may not know it, but her actions are like a dagger to his spirit. Men take those comments and actions extremely personally. Did you notice that Troy said, "She doesn't like my sperm"? That's a part of him, something he cannot change. So he hears, *You're a loser.* And he feels that his wife doesn't love him, that he can't win.

One woman asked us, "But what if my husband is not that good in bed?" If a wife has difficulty experiencing orgasm, if she does not feel the tingly sensations that come with foreplay, if she's bored by sex, then she needs to communicate with her husband—but in an affirming, encouraging way. Blurting out

"Just forget it. This isn't working," in the middle of sex is not the way to do it. Instead, say something like, "I love you, and I'm so attracted to you. I want to experience the best sex I can with you. I want you to make me scream out in passion. I'm just not there yet. Will you help me?"

That does several things. First, it says, *I want you.* Second, it respects a husband's self-esteem. Third, it gives him a problem to fix. Remember, men love to fix things. And if a wife calls on her husband to help her "fix" her sexual response, he very likely will take on the role with seriousness.

How to Meet Your Husband's Need for Affirmation

Wives, here are some ideas to get you started in meeting your husband's need for affirmation.

1. Affirm him for who he is. Affirmation starts outside the bedroom. It's a lifestyle, not a technique. Let your husband know that you value him. When you admire him, say it out loud. When he makes a decision that took courage, recognize it and commend him. Notice when he shows perseverance in his work, and say something about it. Help your husband know all the good things you see in him.

2. Affirm him for being a good lover. Tell your husband what you like about the way he loves you. Tell him what you like about his body. If you aren't sure how to do this, ask your husband for advice: "I want to affirm you as a lover, but I want to do it right. How can I best tell or show you what a great lover I think you are?" We can guarantee that not one man will rebuff such a question!

3. Practice the Golden Rule. This is one place where the Golden Rule works well. Treat your husband the way you would want him to treat you. Talk to (and about) him the way you would want him to talk to (and about) you. It's that simple. Become lavish with your praise and admiration.

4. Understand that for men, body image does matter. A man's body image is important to him. As men age, their bodies change. Their muscle tone diminishes, they begin to lose their hair, and they have a harder time staying in shape. A husband loves to hear that his wife is impressed and turned on by looking at his body, by holding or fondling him. Since a wife is typically not stimulated visually, she probably is not that aroused by viewing her husband's body. But a husband needs to know that his wife likes what she sees, that he's "got what it takes" to be her one and only. This may be a stretch for some women, but when a wife makes an affirming comment about her husband's body, his confidence soars.

Part Two

ENRICHING YOUR SEX LIFE

CHAPTER 8

When Your Libidos Don't Match

Throughout this book we have shared stories of couples who've had problems in their marriages because the sex drives of the husbands and wives were not always on the same level. In most situations, the husband's drive is stronger than his wife's. We've offered suggestions for how couples can change their attitudes and behavior and can grow in their ability to love and serve each other in ways that will bring balance and satisfaction to their sex lives.

Sometimes, though, we need to look beyond attitudes and behavior to other factors that can contribute to sexual problems. When God created males and females, he gave them a physiological drive to have sex with each other, to procreate. Our bodies' vehicles for regulating and arousing that sex drive are hormones, which differ in male and female bodies. Typically male bodies have more testosterone—the arousal hormone—which moves consistently through their systems. Female bodies also have testosterone, but not as much. As a result, females usually do not have the same level of desire for sexual release as males do. That's not good or bad; it's simply different. Because of the different levels of testosterone, the male is usually the initiator in sexual activity; the female is usually the responder. It's another way in which God made males and females to complement each other, to work together to form a whole.

UNDERSTANDING THE POWER OF TESTOSTERONE

As testosterone builds physiologically in a male's body, his anticipation of sexual connection also grows. It's as if a husband's body goes through a car wash in which every few minutes testosterone washes over his system. He can't stop that from happening any more than he can stop breathing.

Gary Stewart and Timothy Demy, authors of *Winning the Marriage Marathon*, offer insight about the impact of testosterone on a male body:

> Men have ten times as much testosterone as women. This fact often makes the behavior of many men very confusing to women. The male sex drive is fueled by a hormone that turns the most mild-mannered man into quite the aggressive sort when confined in a quiet locale with the wife of his dreams. Testosterone is like an unstable bottle of nitroglycerin. Bump it and it could explode; mix it with the right ingredients and a chemical reaction is sure to ensue. Women are often bewildered by the way their men can wake up in the morning, gaze at their wife beside them, whose breath is less than desirable and whose hair is more than a little disheveled, and still be sexually stimulated. The pure and simple fact is that testosterone builds while the body rests: Testosterone is at its highest level at sunrise.[1]

In his book *The Sexual Man*, Archibald Hart makes similar observations: "Immediately after being sexually satisfied, the normal male may be able to focus elsewhere—for a while. But it is just a matter of time before his thoughts lead him back to sex. . . . Sure, the average man thinks of other things, like football and politics, but eventually all mental roads lead back to one central fixation: Sex. . . . Strong, urgent, forceful, and impatient, the sex drive dominates the mind and body of every healthy male. Like it or not, that's the way it is."[2]

Men were designed to need sexual release. Every man has a sexual rhythm, the amount of time he can go between wanting a physical release. That sexual rhythm is much like any other body rhythm, such as the rhythm of when our bodies need food. All of us have eating rhythms. Yours may be like Gary's. Every morning at about ten o'clock (usually in the middle of a meeting!), his stomach begins to growl, and he knows he needs to eat. What if he grabbed a breakfast bar and Barb said disapprovingly, "You just ate yesterday. Eating is all you think about. What a one-track mind." Would she be right? No. Eating is something God designed us to do regularly. Our bodies tell us it's time to eat. What if after Barb chided Gary, he put down the bar and didn't eat? How long do you think he would last before he grabbed not only the breakfast bar but also a sandwich, chips, an ice-cream sundae, a slice of pizza—then leftover Chinese food, week-old chili, and a spoonful of peanut butter? Don't laugh! Dieters do it all the time! It's called bingeing. And usually the food we binge on isn't the most healthy for us.

Wives, your husbands need to release the buildup of testosterone. If they don't have sex, their bodies will release testosterone through "wet dreams," or nocturnal emissions. But sex is much more enjoyable. If husbands don't get that release from their wives, they can last for a while. They may show irritability, frustration, isolation, but eventually they may binge and do something that both of you regret.

We've heard countless women say, "That's not my problem. It's my husband's responsibility to stay faithful in this marriage." We do not deny that is true. But think about this for a moment. God created the covenant of marriage, in which one man and one woman stay connected with each other for a lifetime. That means a wife is her husband's *only God-honoring* sexual outlet. What does she communicate if she denies him that outlet? "I won't give to you, but I expect you to stay faithful to me." Do you see how unfair and cruel that is?

A wife is her husband's *only God-honoring* sexual outlet.

Wives, when your husbands approach you for sex, think about what he is saying about *you!* He desires *you*. He wants to become vulnerable with *you*. He wants to share the most intimate relationship a person can have with *you*. Respect his need for you. Encourage him. The worst thing you can do is to shame your husband or say, "All you care about is sex." Love him sacrificially, even if you are not always in the mood.

In their excellent book *When Two Become One*, Christian sex therapist Christopher McCluskey and his wife, Rachel, both life coaches, offer these words: "Consenting to lovemaking at these times should be different [from] just 'going through the motions.' Even though your libido may not be revved up, you can still be an active participant in *loving* your husband; don't dutifully give him your body while your heart and mind check out. Some of what he may need is the emotional connection with you that he finds easiest to make during lovemaking. When he gives himself to sexual enjoyment, you are seeing your husband at his most vulnerable and transparent."[3]

Even though many wives do not feel the "need" for sex as often as their husbands do, most women say that when they give physically to their husbands, they enjoy the sexual experience and their husbands become more emotionally present for them. When a husband and wife get aroused and have orgasms, they enjoy the experience. That's the way God designed it!

Orgasms themselves are very beneficial. Christian sex therapist Shay Roop offers nine reasons why orgasms are good for you:

1. Orgasms boost your mood. They increase your serotonin and endorphin levels, those "feel good" brain chemicals.
2. Orgasms help you relax. Climaxing releases oxytocin, a relaxing/bonding chemical in the brain that reduces stress.
3. Orgasms chase away the sniffles. They boost your immune system by increasing lymphocytes that fight infection.
4. Orgasms tone your muscles. Yes, this is true! Especially a woman's pelvic floor, which controls the flow of urine and is involved in childbirth.

5. Orgasms maintain estrogen levels. Estrogen has numerous functions, including keeping skin supple and elastic, protecting bones, and improving memory and mood.

6. Orgasms increase desire. Climaxing increases testosterone levels. What you don't use, you lose.

7. Orgasms prevent soreness. They flush lactic acid and other waste products from your muscles, which keeps them healthy and free from cramps.

8. Orgasms relieve sexual tension. Having our sexual needs met by our spouses guards against a "wandering eye."

9. Orgasms get you closer. It's the ultimate physical union you can share with your spouse.[4]

WHEN SEX DRIVES DIFFER SIGNIFICANTLY

Most of you who have been married for a number of years know that your sex drives fluctuate. That often means that at certain times in your marriage, one of you has a higher sex drive than the other. This can cause conflict because one spouse wants to have sex, but the other does not always share the same level of eagerness. We hear countless stories from husbands and wives whose marriages are troubled because of conflict over how often they have sex.

As we've already said many times in this book, husbands generally have the more active sex drive because of their higher testosterone levels. But that is not always the case. Some experts indicate that in up to 30 percent of the marriages they surveyed, the wife had the higher sex drive.[5]

What accounts for these differences, and how do you handle them in your marriage? What can you do if you have a diminished sex drive? Before we answer those questions, we'd like to share two stories with you.

Nineteen years into her marriage, Ellie hit a wall. She and Jerry had always enjoyed sex, and even though she was struggling with a chronic illness, they made love a few times a week. But she felt as if her sex drive was in neutral. She lost interest in sex, and it began to affect their marriage. When Jerry would suggest that they make love, she would find an excuse. As is the case with many couples, the spouse with the lower libido dictates the amount, time, and circumstances of lovemaking. Ellie knew that making excuses wasn't the right thing to do, and she blamed herself for not being eager to enjoy sex with her husband.

When Ellie talked with her female internist about her low libido, the physician shrugged it off and told Ellie not to worry. "Worrying only makes it worse." Several months later, Ellie discussed the issue with her gynecologist, also a woman, and asked if the physician would check her hormone levels. The gynecologist replied, "That's not necessary. Sexual responsiveness is all a matter of the mind. Go to a bookstore and buy some erotic books. That will help." Ellie left the appointment frustrated. Not only did she disagree with the gynecologist's advice, but she was also irritated that the two physicians had been so dismissive.

Several years later, Ellie went to a naturopathic clinic for some treatment for her chronic illness. In the course of the intake appointment, Ellie mentioned her low libido. This time the doctor ordered tests to determine her body's hormone production, and the results were significant in addressing

Ellie's concerns. The doctor reported, "It's very understandable that you have a low sex drive. The tests that we ran on your adrenal system indicate that it has nearly shut down. Not only are your levels of progesterone and testosterone very low, but the precursors to these hormones are also very low. We can help you."

Ellie was so relieved. She didn't need to blame herself. It wasn't her fault that she couldn't get aroused as often as she and Jerry would have liked. The doctor gave Ellie bioidentical hormones, which over time balanced her adrenal system and not only helped her chronic illness but also improved her sex drive. It's sad that Ellie spent so many years discouraged, blaming herself for something that had a physiological origin.

Gary had a similar experience. Several years ago, after a surgery that affected Barb's hormone levels, she sought treatment from an internist who specializes in hormone-replacement therapy. The hormone treatments were going so well that Barb began to explain to the physician some of the worrisome symptoms she'd noticed in Gary: fatigue, inability to concentrate, lack of motivation, and others.

The physician said, "From the sounds of it, I think something is amiss with Gary's adrenal system." So Barb began to pray that Gary would agree to meet with the physician and get tested. She told Gary that she loved him and wanted the best for him, and she encouraged him to meet with her physician.

Gary reluctantly agreed. When the doctor talked with Gary about the test results, she said, "Gary, you have some major problems, but I can help you. I'm not going to turn you back into a twenty-five-year-old, but your body will have what it needs to function more normally again." Over time she was able to replenish his diminishing hormone levels. Gary feels great and has regained a general sense of well-being.

FACTORS THAT AFFECT YOUR SEX DRIVE

These two stories illustrate several factors that influence husbands' and wives' sex drives.

1. Hormone imbalance. Both Ellie's body and Gary's were not producing adequate levels of certain hormones. Our bodies are fearfully and wonderfully made, and hidden depletions can cause large-scale physical imbalances that can affect your sex drive—and your marriage. If you suspect you have an imbalance, get help. You may need to persist until you find someone who will test your hormones, as Ellie found. But the persistence is worth it. Don't use hormone substances without your doctor's involvement; hormones function in a delicate balance that should be monitored by a physician. Many times, sex is the last thing that prompts a man to recognize a hormonal imbalance. It's usually several other factors, as it was for Gary.

2. Illness. In Ellie's case a chronic illness contributed to her low adrenal function, which led to a low libido. Our bodies are intricately made, and what is happening in one part of the body affects many other parts as well. Spouses who lack sexual interest may also suffer from thyroid imbalance, an onset of diabetes, heart disease, hardening of the arteries, or many other illnesses. These definitely need the attention of medical professionals. Physicians can use blood tests and other diagnostic tools to detect conditions that may affect your libido.

If your spouse is ill, you and your marriage have a special

challenge. The ill person needs to do everything he or she can do to regain health, and the other spouse needs to find ways to support the ill husband or wife and make allowance for the illness. Jim and Sarah share some insights from their experience coping with Sarah's debilitating immune-system illness.

"Jim is sensitive to my illness and has backed off from initiating sexual contact, which was good at first because it relieved some of the pressure for me. But now it's up to me to initiate when I feel well enough. . . . I want to bring Jim pleasure, but it is such hard work [because I am so debilitated]. I decided this was as much a spiritual problem as a physical, sexual one, so I have prayed and asked for guidance. Many times in marriage the Lord has enabled me to lay down my body for my husband or our children, and I asked the Lord to help me truly minister to Jim in our sexual experience. . . . Slowly I am learning to initiate times of intimacy, even when my own sex drive seems nonexistent. As a result of trusting God and choosing to minister to Jim, we have experienced times of deep closeness, pleasure, and peace. . . ."

Jim . . . concurs, "God has helped Sarah and me to find a path through our sexual struggles. I found it was important to confess my anger and frustration to God and ask for help. And he has been faithful. I think it's also important to be aware that while a husband and wife are redefining their sexual lives because of illness, they are on guard not even to get close to any situation in which they could be tempted. We can respect our spouse's limitations and our marriage by choosing not to use the illness as an excuse for infidelity of mind or body."[6]

3. Medications. Ellie also found that several medications she was taking for her illness affected her libido. That may be a factor for you as well. Some medications that are commonly known to affect libido include certain antidepressants, certain medications used to lower blood pressure, some cholesterol-reducing medications, and many others. If you think your medications may be a factor in your sex drive, talk with your doctor. One woman expressed real pain about her husband's lack of sexual interest: "Because my husband is on medications that decrease his libido to almost zero, I often feel unwanted. My already unstable body image crumbles when my husband has no desire for me. I naturally assume it is me or my body that turns him off. Even though I know the meds are the culprit, I can't help but feel undesirable, especially when I ask for sex and he won't give." If you identify with this couple's experience, be patient with each other but also work toward finding "a path through your sexual struggles," as Jim put it.

4. Stress. We all face stresses, whether they come from our jobs, the challenges of caring for a family, conflict, or any number of other areas. Stresses can be physical, emotional, mental, and spiritual. These stresses, which are part of our modern lifestyle, can deplete our bodies in ways that affect our hormone levels, which can profoundly lower our sexual responses. Gary realized that his hormone depletion stemmed in part from a stressful period after his father's death, a time that demanded a lot from him personally and professionally.

Recognize that stress can interfere with your sex drive. Take care of your body, mind, and spirit. Get exercise. Build margin into your life, taking time for refreshment and replenishment. Meditate on Scripture. If stress is a serious threat to your sex life, seek professional counseling.

5. Depression. Sometimes a lack of sexual interest can be the result of depression, which can deplete hormones. Men and women handle depression differently. Men often don't recognize or understand it, and because they aren't as comfortable as women are talking about feelings and emotions, the depression can go undiagnosed for years. Here again, if depression is a possible factor, contact a physician who can diagnose and treat it. As we mentioned, some antidepressants can suppress your libido, so talk over your options with your physician.

6. Age. Fluctuation in your sex drive may be the result of age. Most males reach a sexual peak during their late teens and twenties, while females commonly reach their peak a decade or two later. That factor alone can account for mismatched libidos and relationship frustration. Extend grace to yourself and each other. Recognize that age affects your sex drives and learn to adjust your expectations.

7. Pregnancy and childbirth. The hormonal changes related to pregnancy and childbirth can also affect sexual desire. Nursing mothers' hormones, including those that influence sex drive, fluctuate through the months of nursing, and a mother's limited enthusiasm for sex can effectively cool her husband's desire as well.

8. Unresolved conflict. Sometimes a lowered sex drive is the result of emotional issues, and conflict heads the list of emotional factors that can diminish the sex drive. When husbands and wives argue and have conflict, it's hard for them to turn off their feelings and hop into bed. Or they may try to fight back by withholding sex because they are upset about money, the kids, or any number of other issues.

In our book *Healing the Hurt in Your Marriage*, we help couples recognize the "open loops"—the unresolved conflicts—that affect their relationships. These conflicts result from the offenses that blindside us, the anger that kicks in when our spouses wound us, or the arguments that don't seem to stop. When conflict is unresolved in a marriage, spouses may try to avoid sex.

When conflict is unresolved in a marriage, spouses may try to avoid sex.

Husbands and wives often deal with these conflicts differently. In many cases wives will sort through their pain and resolve it through the connection with their husbands. Women will talk about the conflict, feel it, express it, and get to the other side. At other times wives may feel so wounded by a conflict that they withdraw from their husbands and are not open to sexual contact. Husbands often find it harder to process a conflict and get to the other side. When there is an open loop, they often become frustrated and angry, and will spend energy trying to "fix" or solve the conflict. When that doesn't work, they withdraw and become isolated, internalizing the anger. Eventually the suppressed anger results in ulcers, headaches, stress, and even depression.

Our friends Jim and Carol Anderson-Shores have conducted dramas at events where we have spoken. They perform one sketch that effectively illustrates this scenario. Carol is brewing up emotion over losing a research card for a report she is writing. Jim, who beforehand wanted to connect to her, loses interest in connecting to her as he begins to assimilate her anxiety, stress, and frustration. She vents, he personalizes. She rants, he tries to fix it. And when she finds the card, she wants a kiss, and he rejects her. When she asks, "Why are you rejecting me?" he answers, "I don't know, but when I figure it out, I will tell you." Perfect illustration. In the drama, Jim is demonstrating his lack of awareness of the unresolved conflict and can't shift gears as quickly as Carol. He just knows "something is wrong."

Spouses wounded by conflict find it hard to engage in sex and other forms of intimacy. Learn to recognize your unresolved conflicts and work toward closing the loop by talking about them, forgiving each other, and rebuilding your trust.

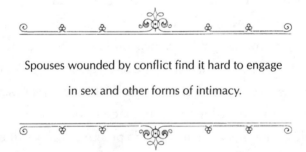

Spouses wounded by conflict find it hard to engage
in sex and other forms of intimacy.

9. Unresolved emotional issues. Sometimes spouses' sex drives are diminished by unresolved issues such as sexual abuse or betrayal or infidelity or pornography. These are serious issues that can deeply affect sexual interest and activity. We think they are so important that we devoted an entire chapter, chapter 13, to discussing these issues more fully and offering hope and help.

Another emotional issue that can affect your sex drive is guilt. Are you hiding something? Are you having an emotional or sexual affair? Are you struggling with lust or homosexual feelings? Are you masturbating? Self-stimulation can block your ability to respond to your spouse as you step into deception and self-pleasure. Even though you will experience the physical release from self-stimulation, you may find an emptiness in your soul, spirit, and heart. Quick release often brings quick guilt and shame.

10. Erectile dysfunction and premature ejaculation. Men put a lot of stock in their sexual performance. If they feel they can't deliver, then they will avoid the embarrassing situation altogether. What a husband often fails to realize is that at some point most men will experience premature ejaculation or the inability to have an erection. That doesn't make him any less of a man or fantastic lover. Wives, if your husband struggles in either of these areas, be patient and affirming. Never diminish him or criticize his performance. Unfortunately many men have tried to "cure" erectile dysfunction by getting a prescription for Viagra or a similar drug, but that's not necessarily the solution—that's the bandage. Many times the solution can be as simple as increasing testosterone levels.

How Can You Cope with Mismatched Libidos?

Most couples find that their sex drives are not perfectly aligned. At various times throughout marriage, for all of the reasons we've just outlined, one of them has a lower drive to have sex.

How can you successfully navigate those times? Read through the following suggestions, and pick one or two that will work for you.

1. Appreciate what you have. Look for the good in the relationship. Rather than bemoaning the deficiencies, gratefully accept what is. Affirm your spouse. Every time you think of something you love about your husband or wife, say it—out loud—so that both of you hear the encouraging words. Compliment and build your spouse's self-esteem.

2. Pray for each other. If one of you is struggling with a low sex drive, pray, asking God to give you patience and understanding. Ask him to bless your spouse. Ask him to help you both find creative ways to express and experience a satisfying sexual relationship.

3. Express your desires. If you have the higher sex drive, learn to communicate your sex needs without nagging or demanding. Tell your spouse that you want to be close to him or her, that you want to stay out of the danger zone, that you want to experience a deeper level of intimacy. The many suggestions in chapter 10 will help you talk about your sex needs.

4. Meet your spouse's need. One man told us that he was struggling with a low libido and it was frustrating his wife. He realized if he didn't do something about it, he could place his wife in danger of going outside the marriage to find fulfillment. He told her, "I'm struggling. My sex drive isn't what it should be, and I don't know why. But I love you as my wife, and I don't want to cause you to step into a sinful situation. Since your libido is higher, let me take care of your need." He helped his wife climax, and as he did, he often found that he became aroused too. But even if he hadn't, he still could love her, serve her, and take care of her need.

Remember that not every lovemaking session needs to result in both of you having an orgasm. That's a great goal, but it may not happen every time. The important thing is to stay close to each other, to communicate your love in both physical and verbal ways, and to stay committed to meeting each other's needs.

How to Get in the Mood When You're Not

So, what can you do if you have a lower sex drive than your spouse does? After giving attention to any of the factors that we discussed earlier in the chapter, you can try a few of the suggestions outlined below.

1. Pray. Ask God to heighten your sexual desire for your husband or wife. If you don't initially feel comfortable doing that, remember that God created sex drives, and he wants you to experience the pleasure that comes from enjoying a satisfying sex life with your spouse.

2. Shape your attitudes. According to Christian sex therapist Douglas Rosenau, "Sex is 80 percent imagination and mind and 20 percent friction."[7] The mind is the command center for all sexual feelings. Thousands of thoughts go through your mind in a day, determining how you see yourself and what you do. How do you think of yourself as a lover? If you primarily think, *I really don't care much for sex; it's not that exciting* or *I hope he [or she] doesn't want sex tonight* or *Sex is just another chore,* then you're not going to be in the mood. Although you may claim that you can't help it, we believe you can choose to change those thoughts. Your feelings and attitudes come from your thoughts.

So think about the intense sexual pleasure and freedom that God intended for a husband and wife. Think about how wonderful it is that your spouse desires and pursues *you*. The more you think about yourself and your spouse as people to whom God has given sexual drives and needs, the more you will be open to sex with your spouse.

3. Pay attention to sexual desire. If you have a low sex drive, then train yourself to become aware of the slightest feeling of sexual desire. These can be significant starting points. If the feeling hits, go with it. Don't dismiss it. Mention your desire to your spouse, and if it's appropriate and possible, act on your desire. It will be a great encouragement to both of you.

4. Remember past experiences. If you feel that your sex drive is in neutral, think about times when you and your spouse had great sex. What made it exciting? Will replicating that experience help you feel aroused again? Replace negative attitudes with positive memories. Remember why you fell in love. Think about the times when your sex life sizzled. Then try to recapture that.

5. Just do it! As we say elsewhere in this book, sometimes it's good to take the Nike approach and just do it. Just have sex, even if you are not particularly in the mood. Of course we don't mean to suggest that you become sex slaves or that you allow yourself to feel used. But just as we do things we don't particularly want to do in many other areas of our lives, at times it makes sense to engage in sex even if we're not all revved up. Be sure to have the right attitude, however. This is not the time to think, *Okay, I'll just grin and bear it, and give him [or her] some pleasure.* This is the time to remember that we are called to serve each other with self-sacrificing love. That's the kind of love Jim and Sarah showed each other during Sarah's illness, as we discussed earlier in the chapter. Times of lowered libidos are opportunities for couples to demonstrate Christ's love to each other by honoring the other's need and putting it before their own.

6. Exercise. Exercise isn't just for your health! Research confirms that even moderate exercise raises endorphins and may increase the intensity of sexual arousal. Make regular exercise, even if it is only walking twenty minutes three times a week, a part of your plan to heighten your sex drive. If it's possible, walk together. Find a park or walking trail that allows you to be inspired by nature, and then use the walking time to talk about your day, your joys, and your challenges.

7. Do things that appeal to your senses. Psychologists tell us that our senses have a powerful influence on sexual experiences. First, pay attention to your sense of *smell.* Mental associations of a certain smell can take you back to distant memories, change your attitude, calm and invigorate you. Find a candle with a scent that you wish to associate with times of sexual intimacy. When your spouse wants to have sex and you're not in the mood, light the candle and give yourself time to let the association kick in. Perfumes, cologne, or scented lotions may have the same effect.

Second, be aware of your sense of *touch.* If a gentle massage will help you, make that a part of your routine. Ask your husband or wife to use oil or a scented lotion to gently rub your body, beginning on your shoulders and back but then moving to erogenous zones that may increase your sense of sexual arousal. Then relax and enjoy the sensual pleasure.

Third, pay attention to your sense of *sight*. If you are visually stimulated, ask your husband or wife to help by wearing clothing—especially underwear—that appeals to you. Or ask him or her to shed that clothing to help you become aroused. Try having sex in different locations, with different lighting. Once you have made sure that you will have privacy, make love on a blanket near a mirror or in front of a crackling fire in a fireplace. Have sex on the living room floor. Try it outdoors, whether it's on a covered deck during a thunderstorm or in a private place on a sunny afternoon. The point is, use your imagination and your sense of sight in ways that will contribute to your arousal.

Finally, be aware of how the sense of *hearing* can contribute to your sex drive. Music can arouse the body. Find a CD that puts you in the mood, and play it only when you are sexually intimate. Soon you will associate the music with a pleasant sexual experience.

CHAPTER 9

When You Are Too Exhausted to Have Sex

When Bart pulled into his driveway at six-thirty in the evening, he was bushed. Twelve hours earlier he had driven into the lot at Zingle's Chevrolet, where he works as a senior service writer, and had seen eight vehicles already waiting in line. He felt behind before he even started his day. All day long he dealt with a steady stream of impatient and cranky customers. The day had been so hectic that he hadn't even had a chance to answer his cell phone or connect with his wife, Beth, just to say hi.

As he approached his house, he wanted nothing more than to kiss his wife, grab something to eat, slip into oblivion on the couch, and watch CNN and ESPN. He hoped Beth had a good meal prepared. He was hungry. Bart stepped onto the back porch, but instead of being greeted by the smell of cooking food, a flustered and annoyed Beth met him at the door.

"You're late," she said, thrusting a slip of paper at him.

"What's this?" The paper had directions and phone numbers listed.

"We don't have time," she said. "You didn't answer your cell phone. You were supposed to pick up the Jackson twins and take Lilly and them to soccer practice. Then you need to pick up Jonathan from his drum lessons and take him to youth group."

"Hold on!" Bart said. He was not eager to spend his evening transporting kids around. "Why don't you take them?"

"Because," she said, exasperated, "Joey needs to get to his baseball game in ten minutes or the coach won't let him play. It's our turn to carpool. I have to pick up Zach and Todd and Sam too. They're waiting for me. Then I have my Bible study meeting, and . . ."

Bart felt a glaze spread over his brain.

"Joey! Come on, let's go!" She turned and grabbed her purse, then reached up to kiss her husband.

"Sorry, sweetie," she said, a little softer. "This is only for a season."

"It feels like a never-ending season," he muttered, dodging his son as he ran downstairs and out the door.

"Just grab something to eat at Taco Bell if you get a chance," Beth yelled as she climbed into her car. "See you tonight. Love you!"

Bart sighed, dropped his tote onto the kitchen table, and walked back out of the house.

Later that night, Bart was lying in bed, waiting for Beth to finish brushing her teeth in the bathroom. Several moments later, she turned off the light and slipped into their bed. She snuggled up to him, and he could feel her silky nightgown rub against his thigh.

Something flickered in his brain. *That used to get me excited.*

Bart and Beth were so stressed and exhausted that they hadn't made love in weeks. He'd lost track of how long it had been. And, he had to admit, it didn't seem to bother him anymore—or her, for that matter. He was exhausted, but his mind kept whirling. *Why is our life so out of control? We don't make love anymore—and we don't even care. Is this what the next fifty years are going to be like?*

SEX'S NUMBER ONE ENEMY

Multitudes of sex therapists and marriage counselors name fatigue as the number one enemy of sexual intimacy. When couples are worn out, sex is one of the first things to go. Typically, the early honeymoon years of highly charged sexual lives come to a screeching halt in the child-rearing years.

The television poster couple for this kind of exhaustion is *Desperate Housewives'* Lynette and her husband. In one of the first episodes of the initial season of the ABC drama, we see how incredibly exhausted they are. Lynette and her husband have four children, several of whom suffer from ADD. One day Lynette's husband comes home from a business trip, clueless as to how tired and worn-out she is from caring for and chasing after kids all day. When he indicates that he wants to have sex, she asks, "Do I have to *do* anything?" She's just so exhausted! Finally they're in bed, and she's concerned about birth control. He doesn't have a condom, so he says, "Let's just risk it." Risk it with four kids who are driving her nuts? She doesn't think so. She hauls off and decks him!

That scene shows an all-too-important issue for many couples.

We're so busy and overextended and exhausted that we simply don't have time to do the things we need to or used to enjoy doing. So where do we find room to enjoy each other if everybody else is stealing all our energy?

In a *Redbook* article, author Susan Crain Bakos states that "an estimated 24 million American women say they don't have time, are too exhausted, or just aren't in the mood for sex."[1] They have work stress, kid stress, household stress, pressure to win in the marriage, the church—and on and on. So when a husband wants sex, a wife often sees his needs as the enemy. Not that *he* is the enemy; his sexual needs are.

"I never thought sex would be a problem in my marriage," Christine said. "I loved sex when we first got married. Sex used to connect my husband and me. Now it divides us. After rearing three kids, keeping up with meals and the house, being a youth group leader, working, and taking care of my parents, sex is the last item on my list. It isn't that I don't love or want him; I'm just exhausted. From the minute I wake up, I face demands from my kids, employers, clients. By the time I get to my husband, I have nothing left to give! I don't want my husband to feel distant or get upset every day I say no to him, but I don't have a choice. I'm too beat."

One of the typical differences between how men and women experience exhaustion is that even when a man is weary, he can usually find *just enough* energy to have sex. Not so for a woman. When she is exhausted, even the thought of having sex can make her want to pass out. Because a woman's arousal mechanisms are more complex, sex takes more time and energy for her. She enjoys sex, but she may feel that the effort isn't worth the climax at the end. So when a wife thinks, *Do I have to do anything?* it isn't a reflection of her husband's lovemaking skills. It's more a reflection of how exhausted she is.

Why is it that when we become overworked and stressed, we let slide those things that are most healthy for us? Prayer, time alone with God, our spouses, and ourselves. Exercise, eating healthy, sex. If sex enters our minds—even fleetingly—we think, *I'd really like to have sex, but when do I have the time and the energy?*

The truth is that we *need* sex to stay healthy. But sex should not be something we give because we have to. We need to give because we *want* to, because the benefits are so great, and because above everything else, we are committed to our marriages. Let's face it: If we fail at doing everything we can for our marriages, the rest is moot. Often we hear people say, "I'm the only one who can be a mother [or father] to my children." You know what? They are right. But even more important is that *you* are the only one who can be your spouse's lover. You are the only one who can meet your spouse's sexual needs. It may "take a village" to raise a child, but it takes you and you alone to meet your spouse's sex needs. After God, the most important relationship commitment in your life is your spouse. Period. Not your children. Not your work. Not your schedule, your church work, your agenda.

"*But...!*" we hear you protesting. You owe it to your children to have a great marriage. That's where their security is the strongest. That means you and your spouse must find time in your harried, hurried, overscheduled lives to have sex regularly.

You are the only one who can meet your spouse's sexual needs.

MAKING SEX A PRIORITY

We know a husband and wife who both work and have commutes of more than thirty-five minutes. Every morning, the wife is up at five o'clock to wake their three-year-old son and get him ready to go to her sister's house for child care. She drops him off on her way to work.

One day as the husband and wife were talking to us about how disconnected they felt from each other, we mentioned that they needed to take a weekend away just for themselves. "We don't have time to do a bed-and-breakfast," the wife scoffed. "I'm already too swamped. We have to run errands on the weekends. Besides, we don't have a lot of money, and I can't ask my sister to take Bradley on the weekend too."

The couple made their dilemma sound justifiable. (Don't we all?) But the truth is that we choose our priorities. This couple is not guarding their marriage. Yes, children come along. Yes, sometimes both spouses need to work. Yes, sometimes you feel as if you can't afford to pay a babysitter.

But at the same time, if your marriage is going to make it, sex is not optional; safeguarding your marriage is not optional. The Bible doesn't say, "So do not deprive each other of sexual relations. The only exception to this rule would be if you are too tired, have worked too hard, have too many commitments, or can't pay for child care." The Bible sees sex as so important that it suggests the only exception to regular sex is when a couple decides to devote concentrated time to prayer. The Bible sees marital sex as a unique privilege, duty, and right.[2]

Gavin and Chondra had a fairly vibrant sex life in the early years of their marriage. Little by little they encountered speed bumps. They had baby Morgan, whose needs moved him to the front burner, leaving Gavin increasingly ambivalent as he sensed that his needs were no longer important. Chondra worked outside the home, rose early in the morning to meet Morgan's needs, tried to take care of the house, and tried to keep all the plates spinning in the air. Gavin's job became more demanding; he was passed over for a promotion, and they experienced more and more financial stress. They were too tired to have sex and were distracted by all the needs in their lives. The connection that seemed so effortless only four years earlier began to unwind before their eyes.

We can push sex to the side and claim that it's "just for a season." But pretty soon, that season turns into a pattern. That's when it becomes ingrained in the heart and we become blind to what we're doing. But the needs for relational and sexual connection do not disappear.

I (Gary) remember when I was working toward my doctorate and was barely home for my family. I was working sixty to seventy hours a week, and Barb and I had become more like roommates than lovers. One day Barb handed me an article about Paul Tsongas, who was a presidential candidate at the time. Tsongas had been diagnosed with cancer, and after taking time for treatment, he announced he was withdrawing from the presidential campaign. Some reporters asked him, "Why? You could go down in history." His reply: "I don't know one man who's ever lain on his deathbed and said, 'I wish I had spent more time at the office.'"

In bed that night after I read the article, I thought, *I wonder why Barb chose this article to give me.* That was the beginning of my realization that I needed to make some tough decisions about my life and my marriage. I had to say no to things in order to bring more balance into our connection time. So Barb and I spent many hours going over our schedules, trying to figure out where to cut back. I quit committees—even prestigious ones I felt would further my career. I had to start saying no to activities that took me away from my family. They were difficult decisions. But little by little, by saying no, some of the resilience came back into our relationship. Soon we began to see a difference in our marriage. Those little decisions added up to successes.

In the lives of overextended couples, the tail is wagging the dog. Life is running them. And for what? Really? You gain the world but lose your marriage, which in essence is like losing a piece of your soul.

Of all sexual issues, exhaustion is the one over which we have the most control. This is the one area in which spouses can help each other regain some sense of balance. How? Either by reprioritizing or working less or saying no to outside activities that don't further the marriage or by asking for help. Making sex a priority sends this message: My time and intimacy— emotionally, spiritually, and sexually—with you is more important than my joining another bowling league and being gone another night every week.

Nothing cuts a husband's pride quicker than knowing he's number twenty-five on his wife's to-do list. And the same holds true when a woman feels last on her husband's priorities list. Be honest for a moment—could you be neglecting your spouse?

MAKING ROOM FOR SEX

Of all of the bedroom busters, exhaustion is one that will require behavioral change. Rebalancing your life demands discipline. It means finding babysitting options. It means choosing to shorten your work hours. It means learning to say no. Here are some ways to begin making changes in order to make your sexual intimacy a top priority.

1. Evaluate yourself. Ask yourself: What am I getting out of this pace? What's the payoff? Does it make me feel good about myself? Am I working for others' affirmation? Am I a pleaser? Am I a perfectionist? Does it keep me independent? Does it keep me in control?

The answers can be key to why you are keeping your spouse at a distance sexually. Some people hide behind the activity. One man told us, "I'm working seventy hours a week because I want to be affirmed. I understand that issue, but to me the payoff is better there than breaking out of that for some potential payoff with my wife."

Marriage calls us to give everything, to commit *completely*. It isn't about the payoff, it isn't about what we get out of the marriage or what our spouses can do for us. Marriage is a choice to live a God-honoring life. It's about growing and maturing spiritually. The only way that can happen is when we understand the sacrifice involved in our marriage commitments.

Marriage calls us to give everything, to commit completely.

If you discover that you are using busyness to avoid intimacy or to hide unresolved conflict, you may need to dig deeper. Don't be hesitant to get professional help to move back to a place of wholeness in your marriage. Chapter 13 tackles some of the deeper issues that you may need to address.

2. Replenish yourself. What activities replenish you? Is it a bubble bath alone at the end of the day? Is it watching a baseball game uninterrupted? Is it a walk alone or a walk through the park with a good audiobook or a relaxing CD? Is it stopping by the grocery store and buying yourself that bunch of flowers? Is it taking thirty minutes a day to read an exciting novel? Is it spending a half hour meditating quietly? Is it driving down to the local café, sipping a skim latte, and writing in your journal? Is it taking that jog along the riverbank?

Replenishing needs to be a daily routine. We know a woman who uses her two-hour commute time to listen to her favorite audiobooks. "I can't explain it," she told us, "but losing myself in a good audiobook makes the commute go faster, makes me a nicer person, both on the road and to my family. It helps me unwind so that when I arrive home, I'm ready to focus on my family."

3. Reprioritize. A couple need to recognize that they have a mutual problem that requires a mutual solution—and that solution may require mutual sacrifice for mutual benefit. Sit down and tackle the problem together. When we asked our survey respondents to tell us what they *disliked* about sex, *fatigue* was at the top of the list for 58 percent of the spouses. In another survey, 80 percent of new moms said their sex life deteriorated because they were simply too tired to make love.[3]

We hear this statement often: "Sex isn't high on my priority list." Quite frankly, many men would shudder at where sex comes on their wives' priority lists. When we conducted a survey for our book *The Five Love Needs of Men and Women,* sexual intimacy ranked thirteenth for women. Some of you may be surprised it came in that high. Well, some people in a Florida study would agree. Their respondents said, "Sex just beats out sewing for pleasure"—at number thirty-seven on the list. Ouch.

Busyness may seem like a "season" of life, but if you don't nurture your sex life now, later may be too late. The further apart a couple grows, the longer and more difficult the path back to intimacy becomes.

From the husband's perspective, he might say, "Well, I'm just looking for sex once in a while. It doesn't take that long." But it isn't just about sex; it's about creating the *environment* of sex and sexual intimacy in marriage. If you want your marriage to be God-honoring, if you want a solid and trustworthy marriage, you need to agree that no matter what, you will carve out time each week just to relax and have fun with each other.

If you want your marriage to be God-honoring, if you want
a solid and trustworthy marriage, you need to agree that
no matter what, you will carve out time each week just
to relax and have fun with each other.

Evaluate your priorities. If making the payments on your
house requires both of you to work, what's more important—
the house or your marriage? Why not move into a smaller house
and focus on your marriage? Who cares what other people
think? A lot of people may weigh their options: *Okay, nice
house—sex with my spouse. Hmm. I'll take the nice house.* To
them it's worth the stress of putting their spouses on the back
burner. But if you neglect the sex, you'll probably be selling the
house in the near future because your marriage will have deteriorated. We know too many people who bought an expensive
house that forced both spouses to work, and they ended up getting a divorce. That's the reality, friends. Something has to
give—or something *will* give. And more than likely, that something will not be without pain and long-term consequences.

Train your mind to understand that saying no to things that
aren't marriage-related is saying yes to your marriage. Often
when we say yes to our children's extracurricular activities, to
being on every church committee, to working extra hours, we
say no to our spouses and to sex. And guess who suffers most

when we do that? Everything and everyone. When we say no to caring for and nurturing our sexual intimacy, ultimately we say no to healthy kids and work and church.

We understand that the pressure is intense to make sure you are giving every opportunity to your children. But your kids may be wearing down too. We have friends who told their kids, "You get one sport a year. Make your choice." It was a shock to everybody's systems, but this couple realized they had to change something or they were headed for a breakdown. Once this husband and wife held their ground, they started to have fun again. They became each other's friend again; they had time for sex. Their marriage and family really turned around.

An overly stressed, busy marriage loses its resiliency. It's like a rubber band that has lost its elasticity. You pull on it a few too many times, it cracks and eventually snaps, rendering it useless. Cutting down busy schedules helps return the elasticity and resiliency to a marriage.

Grab your calendars, sit down with your spouse, and talk through your schedules. Ask each other these questions:

- What is an absolute priority?
- What feels like an absolute priority but really isn't?
- What can we get rid of, at least for this season?
- What is the best day to set aside as our date day—a time for just the two of us to have sex, to have fun, to enjoy each other?

If your family responsibilities cause you exhaustion and busyness, then you need to hire, bribe, or threaten parents, grandparents, neighbors, friends, or church members to babysit your kids

DR. GARY AND BARBARA ROSBERG

so you can get away. Offer to swap child care responsibilities with another couple. But occasionally you need to leave everything behind and go somewhere with your spouse just to have fun and make love. This is a priority, a must.

4. **Schedule regular times for sex.** Scheduling sex is particularly important if you feel overextended. Realize that sex is not going to be as spontaneous as it may have been in your honeymoon years. But your busy schedules mean you need to be intentional and proactive.

Put it on your calendars. Mark off every Thursday night or Saturday morning—whatever works for you—for a month. Get into a pattern; otherwise you aren't going to do it. If that's what it takes for a season, then do it. You need to get yourselves back to remembering, *Oh yeah! This is really fun!*

5. **Put Sabbath back into your week.** God built into his schedule—and ours—a time to rejuvenate. He knew that we would become so caught up with our "important" stuff, that we would neglect times of refreshment and joy.

Sabbath rest was so important to God that he made it one of the Ten Commandments. It's a biggie, friends, right up there with "do not worship any other gods." In fact, it's listed *before* "do not murder" and "do not commit adultery."[4] If God takes rest that seriously, then we need to take it seriously as well.

In an interview with *Marriage Partnership* magazine, author Randy Frazee tells the story of how he went through a period where he experienced insomnia for forty-five days. Finally, after he couldn't take it any longer, he visited his physician, who told him he had a problem with his adrenal system. Randy had been going so long and fast without regular replenishment that his system had gone into overdrive. His physician told him, "You have a choice. Move to Borneo, or make a lifestyle change. If you don't, something serious will happen to you." Randy had discovered that when your body doesn't have time to recuperate, it eventually takes it out on you. Your relationships suffer, your sleep suffers, your sex life suffers.[5]

Our friend Annie told us about a conversation she had with her Jewish friend about sex and the Sabbath. The woman told Annie, "There are certain things I always try to do on the Sabbath. One is that I always have sex with my husband."

"Really?" Annie said. "I thought sex was considered work and that you were not supposed to work on the Sabbath."

"Oh, no," replied the Jewish woman. "Having sex with your spouse on the Sabbath is worth double brownie points to God. You get so many brownie points for all these good things you do. But when you have sex with your husband on the Sabbath, you get *double*." Whether or not God gives brownie points, we all need to understand that God has provided rest, refreshment, and fun when spouses nurture their sex lives. This Jewish woman understands the importance God places on sex.

6. Plan a getaway. Don't use a financial crunch as an excuse. Save up for a getaway! Once every month or so, go somewhere. Go to the motel down the street. Check out priceline.com for hotels in your area. Go to a KOA and rent a cabin. If your friends are going to be away for the weekend, ask them if you can use their house.

Getting away takes creativity and intentionality. One couple found an inexpensive way to catch some alone time together. They signed up their kids for a class or activity, dropped them off, and for that hour or so, they went home and made love. That's intentionality and creativity.

7. **Turn off the television**. One big time stealer is the television. Instead of turning it on in the evenings, why not sit outside and listen to the birds? Take a walk. Go to the bedroom and mess around!

CHAPTER 10

The Elephant in the Bedroom: Talking about Sex

I don't know what to do. My husband and I have been married four years and I have never had an orgasm. So I fake having them. I don't want to tell my husband because it would hurt him. So I lie. I know I'm not doing the right thing. But I'm not sure what to do."

This was an e-mail we received from a woman who listens to our radio program. But it could have been from any number of spouses who say the same thing: I'm unhappy in my sex life, and (1) I've told my spouse, but nothing changes; or (2) I haven't told my spouse because I don't want to hurt him or her. And instead of relief, these couples continue to suffer in silence.

But it doesn't have to be that way! Things change when we begin to communicate clearly about our sexual relationships. Many spouses *think* they are communicating, but most just assume their spouses will read their minds.

Marriage counselor Kevin Leman says he's found that most couples spend 99.9 percent of their sexual relationships making love and 0.1 percent talking about it. He suggests that it should be more like 90 percent making love and 10 percent talking about it.[1]

According to a study in the *Journal of Sex and Marital Therapy*, both women and men believe that the opposite sex isn't interested in discussing the details of bedroom behavior. What's interesting, though, is that these same men and women said open communication about sex was important to them personally. However, most couples rarely communicate clearly about their likes and dislikes in the bedroom.[2]

People will often tell us, "*Talk* about sex with my spouse? That doesn't feel natural." Although many spouses are uncomfortable talking about sex—whether out of frustration or embarrassment—they need to. Why? Because sex is one of the most important parts of a marriage relationship, and when a couple's sexual relationship is out of balance, it affects the rest of the marriage. Because sex will never get better and more satisfying if we don't *communicate* about it.

Although many spouses are uncomfortable talking about sex—
whether out of frustration or embarrassment—they need to.

What Keeps Us from Talking about Sex?

Most of us have not been taught how to talk about sex. Some of you grew up in families where your mom and dad enjoyed sex and taught you healthy things about sex. But others grew up in homes where sex was considered dirty or where parents pretended sex didn't exist. Many parents are uncomfortable talking about sexual matters, so they don't.

As a result, we flounder. We learn about sex in junior high locker rooms, romance novels, and movies. Then we get married and find ourselves unable to adequately express our sexual needs. In many cases, it's not that we don't want to talk about it. It's that we don't know how. We're unsure or fearful of how to bring it up.

Sometimes couples don't talk about sex because they are involved in sinful behavior. If Bob is viewing Internet pornography, then he's not as apt to talk about sex with his wife. If Sally is having intimate discussions with her supervisor or if she's using an Internet chat room to meet her needs for romance, then she probably won't discuss intimate topics with her husband.

Many couples don't talk about sex because they are afraid of conflict. They believe, *If I bring this up, we might get into an argument.*

For a lot of people, communication about sex is the big elephant in the room. We want to acknowledge it, but we tiptoe around it, hoping that if we don't mention it, everything will be okay. But time and experience have taught us that the elephant is still camped out—and starting to edge its way into more of the bedroom. So it's time to recognize the elephant and learn to communicate.

So, how does a husband ask his wife for sex? How does a wife communicate her sexual needs and desires? How do a husband and wife sit down and talk about their sexual relationship?

ASKING FOR SEX

We chuckle when we hear people ask us, "What do I say?" They hem and haw, fumbling until they mutter, "Um, maybe to-night, we can, um, you know . . . " They dance around the topic with euphemisms and vague statements.

How freeing it would be to share a language that is clear, honest, and forthright. How freeing it would be for a wife to be aware of her sexual urges and say to her husband, "Can you meet me in the bedroom in five minutes? I want to have sex." Okay, maybe it doesn't have to be that direct—but maybe it can be.

One husband e-mails his wife messages like, "We haven't had a chance to cuddle and make love for a few days. Think you might be able to save energy for a romp in the sack tonight?" He keeps the invitation open-ended. He's not demanding.

When his wife gets the message, she has time to respond. Sometimes she writes back, "I accept your invitation! Looking forward to it with pleasure," and she prepares for their lovemaking later that night. Other times she writes something like, "Today has been so nutty, and I'm exhausted. This isn't about you, it's just that I am drained. Maybe tomorrow would be better." She is clear about a yes or a no, but she does it in a way that communicates openness, not rejection. Notice that when she says no, she gives a reason and assures her husband that nothing is wrong with him. And she really doesn't say no; she says not today. Clear and honest communication eliminates the second-guessing.

One woman told us about her "sex" pillow. One side says, "Yes, tonight," and the other says, "No, tomorrow." This couple uses a little humor in their marriage, but they are communicating about their needs.

194

Part of communicating about sexual requests is to be free to ask follow-up questions. *No* should never be a stand-alone word in a conversation about sex. In fact, just take the word *no* out of your sexual vocabulary. Replace it with *not now*. If you request sex from your spouse, and your spouse responds with "Not now," then your response becomes, "Then when?" Finish the sentence. Complete the conversation. Don't leave it open to misunderstanding.

CREATING A VOCABULARY OF SEX

A friend of ours, a Christian sex therapist, told us that when she was studying to get her license, she had to become comfortable talking about anything sexual. She had to be able to say any sexual term, phrase, anatomical part, or slang word. Although at first she felt awkward, the more she practiced, the more comfortable she became. That's what you need to work toward with your spouse.

We often tell people to do it until it feels natural. Have sex until it feels natural. Act as if you deeply love your spouse until it feels natural. Talk about sex until it feels natural.

Part of learning to talk about sex is having a vocabulary in which both spouses are fluent. So many times, a wife thinks that if she lights a candle, her husband will understand that she wants to have sex. A husband might think that if he fondles his wife's breasts while she is doing dishes, he's giving a clear indication that he wants to have sex. It's critical for couples to talk clearly and openly. That means having a vocabulary that they both understand.

Spend an afternoon or evening with your spouse, and ask each other: "What are some clear ways we can communicate our need to have sex?" The answers will be fun to discover. You'll learn something new, and you will establish the beginnings of a sexual vocabulary. You may be surprised by some of the suggestions: A husband can say, "You know, honey, I need sex" or "Holding you like this gets me revved up. Are you up for some lovemaking?" or "Hey, how about tonight we mess around?" A wife can say, "I'm craving some time in your arms. Want to see where that leads?" or "I'm going to bed early tonight. If you want to join me, I'm open for some fooling around." Say whatever works for you. Develop your own private vocabulary to express your sexual needs.

When our kids were younger, we would use the code words *danger zone*. When Gary would say, "I'm in the danger zone," I understood that meant, "Girl, I need it, and I need you. Put the kids in the backyard, or take them to the neighbors. We're going upstairs and locking the doors." When I would say those code words, they meant, "Skip watching the news tonight. We need to put the kids to bed early, lock our bedroom door, and make love."

Do what works for you. Get to the point where both of you know the rules and can feel the playful side of talking about sex. As you become more confident in this area, it will become easier.

DISCUSSING THE "STATE OF YOUR UNION"

Honesty time. When was the last time you talked, *really* talked about your sex life with your spouse? Did you know this is the absolute best thing you can do to improve your sexual relationship? It's true.

In his book *Sheet Music*, Kevin Leman writes that part of the reason we don't talk about sex is because we don't want to feel bad and we don't want our spouses to feel bad. "Who wants to hear that they're not good in bed? And who wants to be the one who says it? So what usually happens is that relatively simple remedies go ignored. Some spouses put up with something they don't like for a decade or more because they're afraid to bring it up; they don't want to hurt their spouse. Others have denied themselves something for years because they're too embarrassed to ask for it."[3]

Now is the time to start fresh. Commit to talking with your spouse about sex.

Where do you begin? Well, the best time to talk about sex isn't during sex. You don't put on a negligee, light the candles, play the music, and then talk about what you like or dislike.

Sex belongs in the bedroom, but talking about sex belongs anywhere *but* the bedroom. Because of the delicate, sensitive nature of sex, talking about it needs to take place in a neutral place. Maybe on a porch swing in your backyard. Maybe over a cup of coffee. Maybe in a park. But talking about your sex life should not take place when you are trying to have sex.

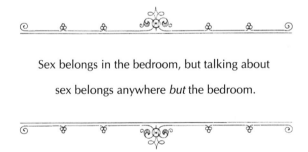

Sex belongs in the bedroom, but talking about
sex belongs anywhere *but* the bedroom.

If at first it's too intimidating, you may want to consider couching it in with other topics, such as when you are discussing other aspects of your relationship and sex is just one part of the discussion. Also, pray before you talk. Ask God to be with you, to help you communicate clearly, gently, and lovingly. Ask him to open your spouse's heart and mind to hearing your concerns and requests. And don't forget to ask him to open *your* heart and mind to hear your spouse's thoughts.

The first several discussions need to be nonthreatening. Take it as cautiously as the more timid spouse needs it to be. We offer several questions, at different levels, to help prime the pump of your communication.

GETTING STARTED

- How did you learn about sex when you were growing up? How was it taught to you?[4]
- What are your three best memories of our sexual interactions over the years?
- Do you think that sex brings us closer, or does closeness lead to sex? Do you appreciate one more than the other?
- What satisfies you most about our sexual relationship?
- Do you enjoy sex with me? What can make it better?
- Is there enough variety in our sex life?
- How often do you want to make love?
- What can I do outside the bedroom to make our sex life more satisfying for you?
- In what type of setting have you always wanted to make love?
- What words or actions throughout the day or week really set the stage for a great time of lovemaking?

GOING DEEPER

- Should we attempt to schedule sex so that we are assured of private time together? How can we make sure that we don't go for too long without sex?
- What excites you the most about me sexually? What do you want me to do to take advantage of that?
- Is sex helpful, comforting, difficult, or anxiety-producing for you when you are under stress? How can our intimacy at those times be at its best?
- Do you ever feel anxious about making love? If so, when and why?
- Do you ever wish that I would initiate sex more often? How would you like me to do it?
- What meets your emotional needs when we're having sex?
- Do we have enough privacy for intimacy? What do we need to do to assure privacy?
- Do you like where we make love? Do you like the ambience?
- Do you like the time of day we usually make love?
- Do you ever feel that I act as if sex is more of a duty than a pleasure? What are some ideas on how that could change?
- Complete this sentence: Five things you could do during the week that would warm me up for sex are . . .

GETTING SPECIFIC

- What three ways would you like to be touched?
- What three things turn you off?
- What three things can I say or do to arouse you?

- Instead of doing _____, can we try _____?
- What sexual positions do you like most?
- Are you experiencing the release you would like?
- What part of my body do you find most exciting? What behavior do you find most exciting?
- How do you want me to talk to you? Would you like me to talk or make more noise during sex, or would you prefer less?
- Am I touching your favorite places?
- Are we trying everything you would like to try?
- What would you like me to do more of?
- If you had all the time in the world, if you had all the energy in the world, if our bed was our playground, what would you want to do with me?
- What do you like best when I surprise you?

It is critical that each of these questions and answers be free from judgment. If one of you says, "I like it when you . . . " and the other reacts in disgust, that will shut down communication fast. Stay open-minded. Listen to your spouse. Affirm and honor his or her courage to talk about sex. If, in the end, you disagree about some things, talk about the differences without hurting each other. The thing to remember is that you're growing together. Speak affirmingly and gratefully.

MAKING COMMUNICATION WORK

∞ **Tip #1: Talk *with* each other, not *at* each other.** Share your feelings about what you are experiencing and what you need. Then listen to your spouse. Be curious. Be a student of your spouse.

∞ **Tip #2: Avoid coarseness and criticism.** Critical comments are a fast way to shut down communication—and your spouse. Do you degrade your spouse—who she is, what he does, how she looks? Do you talk down to her— treat her more like a nuisance than a cherished wife? Show respect and honor in your communication.

∞ **Tip #3: Affirm your spouse.** Make affirmation and appreciation a regular part of your sexual communication. Tell your spouse what he or she does well sexually or relationally. Affirm your spouse verbally.

∞ **Tip #4: Avoid defensiveness.** Be open to what your spouse has to say. Listen without getting defensive. Listen to learn how you can become a better lover. Ask follow-up questions so that you really understand what your spouse is saying.

DISCUSSING THE DELICATE ISSUES

Sometimes delicate issues need to be discussed. For example, if sex has been difficult for you because of a situation in your past or because of a current problem, talk to your spouse about this. Be honest. If your past includes sexual abuse or addiction, or if you are involved in viewing pornography, you need to discuss these issues. They have a huge impact on your marriage. These issues are so important that we discuss them in more detail in chapter 13. If you need to get professional help, don't be too afraid or ashamed to say so.

Other delicate issues could include weight or hygiene, both

of which can affect your sexual intimacy. They are sensitive issues that need to be handled with care and love.

We often hear well-meaning people say such things as, "It doesn't matter if you're overweight. Your husband is so rarin' to go that he won't even notice." Even though to a certain extent that is true, the reality is—for *both* men and women—obesity is something that can get in the way of a healthy sexual relationship. We've received dozens of letters from men and women who plead for help because their spouses are sixty or more pounds overweight. We received a call from a radio listener who said, "What do I do with my husband? He's gained a hundred pounds, and I really want to help him. But I can't find that button to motivate him to lose the weight."

Regardless of whether you are a man or a woman, weight is tied to self-esteem. So if this is an issue that is affecting your sex life and you want to talk about it, first create a safety net. Make sure your spouse does not feel judged or unloved. Without that security, a spouse will feel criticized, which can lead to discouragement, not motivation.

If you are an overweight husband or wife, don't make it your spouse's problem. Take responsibility to change. The reality is, when you don't take care of yourself, it opens a door for your spouse to become visually stimulated by people who do. You need to do everything you can to take care of the body God has entrusted to you. You need to love your spouse—and yourself— enough that you will take care of yourself physically.

Many people have told us what they have not dared to tell their spouses: "It's unpleasant making love to my spouse because he [or she] doesn't smell that great. I wish he [or she] would bathe [or use mouthwash or deodorant] before coming to bed." Friends, this one is an easy fix. Be considerate of your husband or wife. Make sure that your bodies are clean and fresh when you offer them to each other. If you need to talk about hygiene, you might get some ideas from Kevin Leman, who offers this example for approaching the issue: "Honey, so many times, you want to make love to me, but you haven't showered. You don't come to bed smelling clean and fresh, and you know me, I've got a nose like a beagle. I love the smell of your hair when it's just been shampooed. But too often, you smell like work. I love you to pieces, and I love to be with you. It's hard for me to tell you this because I don't want to hurt your feelings, but if you would just shower, that would make me much more willing to please you."[5]

Also, you could suggest taking a bath or shower together, then make a big deal about how wonderful your spouse smells and looks and feels when he—or she—is clean and washed.

The important thing is to be positive and extremely gentle and sensitive.

DISCUSSING SEXUAL BOUNDARIES

Part of the value of talking about your sex life is determining what is acceptable or not acceptable in your relationship. Sometimes a husband or wife would like to try something new but is not sure whether the other will find it exciting or repulsive. The time to introduce new sexual activities is not in the middle of lovemaking. Those need to be discussed outside of the bedroom. Discussing it beforehand avoids embarrassment, shame, or potentially wounding your spouse.

Marriage therapists Louis and Melissa McBurney offer

some guidelines about sexual boundaries in "Christian Sex Rules," one of the most read and requested articles in *Marriage Partnership* magazine.[6] As you discuss what's okay and not okay in your sexual relationship, consider these boundaries:

Keep your marriage exclusive. Part of becoming one in marriage is leaving no room for any third parties. Sex between two people should not be a spectator sport or an opportunity to bring other people into the bedroom, either physically or emotionally. When a marriage loses its exclusivity, it opens the door for mistrust, anxiety, and comparison.

Oprah Winfrey focused one of her shows on a trend that is becoming more and more acceptable to mainstream America. It's called swinging, which involves a husband and wife deciding to spice up their sex life by including other people. Couples go to a club where they have dinner with several other couples and get a sense if these other couples would make a good "fit." Then they trade off partners. If a couple aren't comfortable having sex with others, they can simply watch other couples having sex.

The couples Oprah interviewed were professionals, Brownie troop leaders, Sunday school teachers, stay-at-home moms. They did not feel they were committing an infidelity; both of them agreed to the sex with other couples and were involved in it together. These couples even told Oprah that swinging has strengthened their marriages. They claim that after they dabble with others, they return to their own bedrooms and have the best sex they've ever had.

We believe this is a charade, a lie from Satan. Swinging may seem enticing and fulfilling and exotic, but a few years down the road, these couples will inevitably discover the truth: Cheating leaves us empty and filled with pain. We cannot commit sin with our bodies without damaging our souls because our bodies and souls are inseparable. The apostle Paul addresses this when he writes, "Run from sexual sin! No other sin so clearly affects the body as this one does. For sexual immorality is a sin against your own body. Don't you realize that your body is the temple of the Holy Spirit, who lives in you and was given to you by God? You do not belong to yourself, for God bought you with a high price. So you must honor God with your body."[7]

God designed marriage to be an exclusive, long-term relationship between a husband and a wife. Respecting that design is the only thing that will bring security, trust, and ultimate satisfaction.

Make sure you both agree. Whatever you opt to try has to be acceptable to both partners and has to bring growth to the marriage. If a husband suggests something but his wife just is not comfortable with the idea, we suggest that he defer to his wife's feelings. He should not push her or draw her into areas that either would make her uneasy or would diminish her. This is an issue of respect and honor in marriage. Although it is important to talk about your sexual desires, it is more important to focus on honoring your spouse than on pushing the envelope.

Do only what gives physical and emotional pleasure. Sex should be enjoyable! If it isn't, it may cause resentment and distance between you. Make sure that your sexual activity stays healthy. One Christian couple told us they wanted to experiment with bondage in their sex life. The trouble with bondage or sadomasochistic sex is that it is based in power or domination, not selfless, serving love. Sex should not hurt or cause any pain to either partner.

Continue to have intercourse. Although it is wonderful and fun to try creative ways to give pleasure, unless it is physically impossible for a couple, nothing you do should replace genital union. There is a much stronger bond that occurs between a couple when a husband physically enters his wife.

Guard your relationship. Above all, sex is relational. Make sure that what you do helps you build that relationship. Stay in tune with your spouse—and only your spouse. One of the most dangerous threats to sexual intimacy is introducing sexual fantasies or pornography. They can rob your relationship of the oneness that God designed. In chapter 13 we examine the problems pornography can cause in a marriage and how a couple can overcome them.

CHAPTER 11

Keeping the Fun and Excitement in Sex

During an interview with Christian sex therapists Clifford and Joyce Penner, Neil Clark Warren asked, "What percentage of couples can attain a mutually satisfying sexual relationship?" The Penners responded, "100 percent of them. We've never worked with a single married couple whom we felt were incapable of attaining a high level of sexual satisfaction with each other." They reported that one-third of couples attain this kind of mutual satisfaction quite naturally, without really having to work at it.[1] If you're in the other two-thirds of all married couples, though, you can still reach that high level of sexual satisfaction.

Couples often ask us how to keep the fun and excitement in sex. Our answer: Stay connected. Being connected body to body *and* heart to heart is what makes sex fulfilling and fun. Here are fourteen ways you and your spouse can connect. Try these, then challenge yourself to come up with other fun, creative ideas.

1. Kiss deeply. Do you remember the kind of kissing you did when you first fell in love? Do you still kiss that deeply and passionately? Certainly there's room in a marriage for the peck on the cheek or the quick kiss on the lips. But try getting back to passionate kissing. Take your time. Enjoy the touch and taste of each other's lips. Ask your spouse how he or she would like to be kissed, then practice until you get it perfect.

2. Bask in the afterglow of sex. Savor the closeness you feel after having sex. Stay in each other's arms. Tell your spouse how good it felt and how much you love him or her. Men, if you roll over after sex and snooze, you will miss out on the most intimate time with your wife. Hold her tenderly. Stroke her hair, and tell her you appreciate who she is.

3. Practice good hygiene. This is so simple. Before you have sex, brush your teeth and use mouthwash. Take a shower or bathe. Exploring and holding each other's bodies is much more pleasant when you smell and taste fresh and clean.

4. Create an environment for sex. Set the mood, whether it's candles, music, or the temperature of the room. Think of the mood as a kind of foreplay. If you have children who might enter your bedroom unannounced, put a lock on the door and use it. Keep the bedroom free of clutter and work.

5. Become a student of your spouse's sexual zones. Don't just guess. Ask. Take an afternoon or evening, lie next to each other, and start at your spouse's head. Kiss, stroke, or caress each body part. Ask, "How does this feel? Does it make you tingle? What would make you feel even more tingly—if I caressed less or more?"

One episode of the sitcom *Friends* dealt with the different erogenous zones. Obviously, the characters were discussing sex that is not done in the context of marriage, which, of course, we don't condone. However, the scriptwriters made an interesting point about males and females. Monica and Rachel identified seven erogenous zones. Chandler said, "You're kidding. I thought there were four." One of the women replied, "See, that's your problem. You go one, two, four. You're missing three, five, six. Oh! And toes! Seven." Guys, your wife has more erogenous zones than just her breasts and vagina. Explore with her, and discover where she is most responsive. Although it's good to work toward climax, remember to enjoy the journey along the way as well. It's pretty unbelievable too.

6. **Understand a wife's definition of satisfaction.** "I just don't get it, Gary," Doug told me one afternoon at a conference. "I do everything I can think of in bed, but Jana doesn't always have an orgasm."

"Does that seem to bother Jana?" I asked.

"No, not really," he said. "She seems contented. I don't get that either."

"That's because many women are still satisfied with sex, even when they don't have an orgasm."

Doug stared uncomprehendingly at me. "Huh?"

Husbands, if you want to *satisfy* your wife, you need to shift your definition of satisfaction. Of course, wives love to climax (who doesn't?), but they can still enjoy the lovemaking experience even when they don't reach that peak. As a matter of fact, most women are still satisfied even if they don't have an orgasm every time they make love. Orgasm for a wife is as pleasurable as it is for a husband, just not as necessary for pleasure each time. Most women enjoy the sensuality of cuddling, kissing, and touching every bit as much as the thrill of a climax. Women's sexual plea-sure occurs on many levels other than simply orgasm alone.

Do you know what satisfies your wife? If not, ask her. If cli-max is important to her, make sure you work with her to achieve that goal. Remember how important foreplay is. As we've said before, arousal takes longer for a woman. It means you need to be patient as you focus on her needs for gentle touch, caressing, kissing, as you explore her erogenous zones.

Work out a rhythm with your wife. Is it better to bring her to orgasm first? Do you have simultaneous orgasms? Do you come to climax first and then stay with her to bring her to orgasm? The key is to "stay with your wife" during lovemaking. Even after you have ejaculated, continue to satisfy your wife. If she has not had an orgasm first, continue to stimulate her and observe her cues so that you can progress toward orgasm. Man-ual, direct stimulation of the clitoris outside or inside of the vagina, or oral stimulation (make sure you both agree about this) needs to remain consistent. If this becomes interrupted, the wife will lose the pacing of lovemaking and will not reach orgasm unless she is stimulated again. This doesn't mean she isn't *satisfied*, but it does mean that she probably will not physio-logically experience release.

7. **Understand, accept, and appreciate sexual peaks.** Most men reach their sexual peak in their late teens or early twenties. Most women reach theirs a decade or more later. Often when a woman is in her thirties and forties her sexual desire becomes stronger, sometimes insatiable. And as a man ages, his emotional side grows too. Through each stage, couples grow and learn more about each other and become more patient and sensitive to each

other's needs. This is God's blessing to us because it allows a couple a greater sense of longevity and duration. Many couples miss that, however, because they divorce, not understanding that only through the permanence of lifelong marriage can they develop true intimacy and trust.

8. Understand the different kinds of sex. So often couples feel the pressure to have "perfect" sex—complete with earthquake, fireworks, and multiple orgasms. Not every time you have sex will be a "bell ringer." And that's okay. But you're both connecting. Sometimes sex will be a quickie to meet the need of the moment. Sometimes it will be functional sex, or *just because* sex, when you'll need to think, *I'm not in the mood, but my spouse needs me right now.* Sometimes it may be comfort sex, when life has brought devastation and the only comfort and security are to be found in the arms of your spouse as a lover. You'll be ahead when you understand that the different kinds of sex ultimately point to the ultimate reason for sex: the relationship. The goal is not whether you end with a climax. The goal is that you're connecting as a couple.

9. But make passionate sex the main kind. Don't rush. In our sex survey, we asked women what they hated about sex. Rushed sex ranked number five. When you have a good solid foundation and you've spent years growing together and discovering, then you want to have a lot of variety. But a woman who repeatedly feels unsatisfied, who feels that her husband's pleasure always comes before hers, can feel used and empty. She wants to experience the whole spectrum of what sex covers—the physical, the emotional, the spiritual, the relational.

We aren't saying that rushed or quickie sex is wrong. It isn't.

But sex can't be rushed all the time. That would be like eating nothing but fast food. Going through the local fast-food drive-through for a chili dog and onion rings every once in a while isn't wrong, but your health would suffer if you did that for every meal. Make your goal pleasurable sex that satisfies both of you.

10. Communicate what type of sex you need. If you think you're going to have rushed sex and your spouse is expecting the long, passionate kind, both of you will probably end up frustrated. Communicate your desires and needs. Go back to the fast-food example. If you and your spouse are in the car on your way to eat and she thinks you're going to the steak house downtown, then don't pull into the fast-food drive-through. Clarify your expectations. Remember, women need to prepare mentally for sex. They can do that better if they know what's ahead. If a wife knows that she is headed for quickie sex, she can mentally prepare for that, including the realization that she may not climax. Most of the time she will still enjoy it, even if she may not have the same outcome her husband has.

11. Learn your spouse's sexual triggers. We often joke about his-and-hers sexual triggers. Usually we say that men have one sexual trigger: everything. Women are a bit more complex. But seriously, because men are more visually stimulated, a man can become aroused by seeing his wife naked, undressing, or wearing something provocative. Typically, women are not that way. So a husband needs to discover what his wife's sexual triggers are. What arouses her? The best ways to identify your wife's sexual triggers are by asking her and by observing her response to your lovemaking.

Here are a few categories that may help you understand your wife. Each of them is a foundation stone of connection. Your wife may be a "touch me" girl; she likes hugs and caresses. She may be a "tell me" girl; she likes verbal affirmation and verbal sexual foreplay. She may be a "listen to me and share with me" girl; she opens up after connecting with you through conversation. She may be a "doing" girl; she appreciates it when you pick up messes and help with housework. She may be a "spiritual food" girl; she becomes open to sex after connecting with you through prayer, reading Scripture, and discussing spiritual matters.

12. Keep practicing! Sex stirs the desire for more sex. Love-making elevates the brain chemicals associated with desire. So as we decide to have sex and find we enjoy our time of lovemaking, our libidos increase, often leading to an increased desire to have sex more often.

13. Say "Why not?" When our young grandson asks for something, I (Barb) love to respond with "Why not?" He asks, "Can I have a Popsicle?" and I respond, "Why not?" He understands the response so well that he's begun to mimic me: "Why not, Gaga?" I love that because in a sense I am telling him that I am his greatest cheerleader. Anything he wants, I affirm.

You know what? That is really how I want to be in my marriage. Don't you? I want to be my spouse's cheerleader and affirmer.

What if you started to say "Why not?" to your spouse? Let's say your husband calls you and announces, "I'll meet you at home; we'll enjoy some lunch—and each other." Respond with "Why not?" Let's say your wife e-mails you and announces, "The kids are going to be at sports practice for two hours, starting at 4:30. What if you come home early? I'll make it worth your while." Say "Why not?"

Give yourself permission to enjoy sex. Be open to pleasing your lover. Take on a "Why not?" attitude.

14. Help your wife answer yes to these questions every woman asks. If you can help your wife say yes to these questions, she will feel more eager to jump into your arms.

Will I feel safe and secure? Women long for security the same way men long for success. Your wife feels secure when she's wrapped in your arms. She feels secure when you provide financially for the family. She feels safe when you forgive and accept her. She feels secure when she knows you are faithful to her.

Will I be accepted? A woman needs to know that no matter how she looks or what mistakes she makes, you will stand by her and love her. The key to accepting is forgiveness and consistent affirmation—especially right after she makes a mistake. If she embarrasses herself in front of others, she will immediately look to you for acceptance. If you are laughing along with the others, she will shrivel in pain. Any wife can pick up on her husband's lack of approval.

Will I be appreciated? Your wife naturally wants to please you. She likes it when you are happy with her performance, insight, or advice. She longs to hear, "You did a good job," or "You've worked so hard this week; I want to take you out for dinner so you don't have to cook." Your appreciation motivates her to continue battling those long days. Overwhelm her with appreciation, and watch her sexual desire increase.

Will I feel heard? Most likely your wife works through her emotions by talking, and she needs you to listen. Because you probably use talk to solve problems, you assume that you need to fix whatever it is she is verbally processing. Your skill at solving problems is great when your wife is looking for a logical answer to a problem, but many times she simply wants you to listen. It helps her release stress and see things more clearly. When your wife starts to talk, it's okay to ask her, "Do you need me just to listen, or is this something you'd like me to help you solve?"

Will I feel encouraged? A woman wants to be cheered on by her husband in her desires, interests, goals, and especially her love for God. Study her life. Know what she desires, what is consuming her thoughts, what she dreams about, and what her goals are. Then encourage her at every opportunity.

CHAPTER 12

God in the Bedroom

Some of you might be a bit shocked by the title of this chapter. God . . . in the bedroom? The thought may make you uneasy. After all, isn't sex a private matter?

Most of us think that when we go into our bedrooms, shut the door, and have sex, God somehow closes his eyes. And if we think about the fact that he's watching us having sex, we feel uncomfortable, as if he shouldn't be interested in that part of our lives.

But he is. Not in some voyeuristic way, of course. But let's remember that God *created* sex. It wasn't some cosmic mistake. He masterfully planned it. We may even say it's close to the top of his creation. Creating the stars and the planets and galaxies—sure, that's awesome. Designing the lunar patterns and the ocean tides—very cool. But sex? Now that's the best! He outdid himself.

There's no reason to flinch with guilt or discomfort when you think that God is in the room when you and your spouse make love to each other. We figure that every time a couple makes love and both spouses are responding and actively involved, giving selflessly to the other, God is there cheering: "Way to go!" We envision him smiling and giving high fives to the angels. "I created that," he boasts. "Pretty good, eh?"

It is *very* good.

Just think about these facts for a moment. God provided for human sexuality in marvelous ways. In the *Christianity Today* article "Holy Sex: How It Ravishes Our Souls," best-selling author Philip Yancey explains:

> The human male has the largest penis of any primate, and the female is the only mammal whose breasts develop before her first pregnancy. Virtually all other mammals have a specified time in which the female is receptive, or in heat, whereas the human female can be receptive anytime, not just once or twice a year. In addition, the human species is one of very few in which females experience orgasm, and humans continue to have sex long after their child-bearing years have passed. Why are we so oversexed?
>
> Relationship is the key. Human beings experience sex as a personal encounter, not just a biological act. We are the only species that commonly copulates face-to-face, so that partners look at each other as they mate, and have full-body contact. . . . Having studied some anatomy, I marvel at God laboring over the physiology of sex: the soft parts, the moist parts, the millions of nerve cells sensitive to pressure and pain yet also capable of producing pleasure, the intricacies of erectile tissue . . . the blending of visual appeal and mechanical design.[1]

We are indeed wonderfully made. And somehow we want to keep God out of our bedrooms? We cheat ourselves when we leave God out because he's already in on the whole thing—it was his idea in the first place.

SERVING LOVE

As we've mentioned in earlier chapters, God made husbands and wives to be different. But those differences are not only anatomical; they are internal too. Emotionally, physically, and relationally, we are wired to complement each other. If God designed us this way, then he must have a reason.

Many times we've wondered if God made us with complementary sex needs to help us grow in our ability to serve each other. God's plan for husbands and wives is serving love, a love that focuses on the other.

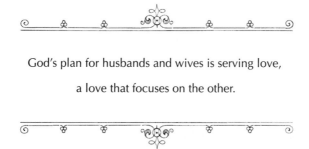

God's plan for husbands and wives is serving love,

a love that focuses on the other.

Serving love propels a wife to study her husband, to understand his sexual rhythm and anticipate and meet his needs. Serving love means the husband is not tackling his wife's "honey-do list" just so he can have sex that night. Serving love compels a husband to act selflessly, to say with his actions, "I love you. I honor you. I cherish you. I want to meet your needs.

I want you to feel safe and secure and comforted in our sex life and our marriage."

But this attitude isn't easy to cultivate. It takes work. It goes against our human nature. In our marriages and sexual relationships, we battle selfishness every single day. We want to have our own needs met first, and we become frustrated when our spouses don't meet our expectations. Our sex lives grow cold, distant, and stale. And in some cases, they die completely. It's as if we are held captive to the pain, anguish, and frustrations of unmet unexpectations. We just can't break free on our own to have an amazing sex life and marriage. We need supernatural help.

I (Barb) was recently reading a Bible passage in which Moses and God were talking. God had chosen Moses to meet with Pharaoh, the leader of the Egyptians. During this meeting, Moses was to demand that Pharaoh free the Israelites, God's people, whom the Egyptians had enslaved for hundreds of years. Moses was anxious about his role as God's spokesman and feared what Pharaoh would do. God responded to Moses by assuring him that when Moses stood before the powerful leader, he would experience a force even more powerful—that of God's hand at work. God wanted to remind Moses—and through this passage, us—of who God is.

This is what God said to Moses: "Therefore, say to the people of Israel: 'I am the LORD. I will free you from your oppression and will rescue you from your slavery in Egypt. I will redeem you with a powerful arm and great acts of judgment. I will claim you as my own people, and I will be your God. Then you will know that I am the LORD your God who has freed you from your oppression in Egypt. I will bring you into the land I swore to give to Abraham, Isaac, and Jacob. I will give it to you as your very own possession. I am the LORD!'"[2]

As I read this passage, I thought about all of the distressed couples Gary and I counsel, couples whose stories are complex. We see so much slavery in marriages today. We see pain and many areas that men and women will not talk about or seek help for because they don't know how. So many couples are in their own private Egypts. They are in bondage, yearning for freedom.

Are you in an Egypt? What is holding you captive? An overcrowded, overscheduled life? Misplaced or unmet expectations? Misunderstandings? Hidden sin? Shame? Pain? Abuse? Trauma? Stress? Fatigue? Pornography? Premarital sex? Mistrust? Deceit? Unforgiveness?

Friend, you need to know that whatever your situation, whatever is holding you captive, God holds the master key for your release. Through his Son, Jesus Christ, he has stepped up to your prison cell, placed that key in the door, unlocked it, and opened it wide for your release. And he looks into your eyes, into your heart and your pain and your slavery, and he says, "You are free."

You need to know that whatever your situation, whatever is holding you captive, God holds the master key for your release.

Too often, though, we don't believe the truth of what God wants to do in and with our lives. Look at the rest of the conversation between God and Moses. After God spoke, Moses went to the Israelites to tell them all he had heard. And instead of believing their leader and feeling joy, the Israelites "refused to listen anymore. They had become too discouraged by the brutality of their slavery."[3]

Too many of us act like the Israelites. We continue in our difficult, miserable, unsatisfying sex lives. We sit in our captivity like prisoners who won't get up, who won't even walk to the cell door and try to get out.

God has opened the cell. He has broken the chains. You are free. *Free.* Don't allow the pain and weight of your burden to keep you enslaved.

Although God has set you free, he will not force you out of your captivity. You must choose to accept your freedom. You can choose Egypt or the Promised Land. *You* can decide whether you want to live like a prisoner or like a victorious, free child of your Creator. God tells us, "Today I have given you the choice between life and death, between blessings and curses. Now I call on heaven and earth to witness the choice you make. Oh, that you would choose life!"[4]

GOD'S PROMISES

If you choose life, if you chose to allow God to release you into new freedom in your marriage and in your sexual relationship, what can you count on him to do?

1. He will free you. When we choose to allow God to lead us, when we willingly give up our desires and our selfishness to enter a relationship with him, when we actively pursue him, he says, "I will free you."

The apostle Paul tells us that "it is for freedom that Christ has set us free. Stand firm, then, and do not let yourselves be burdened again by a yoke of slavery."[5] In our sexual relationships, we are no longer bound by the hidden addictions, the pain, the frustrations. Because of our relationship to God through Christ, those pains, burdens, angers, and frustrations hold no control or power over us.

2. He will redeem you. Because of our relationship with Jesus Christ, God says, "I will redeem you."

In the Old Testament book of Joel, God, speaking through his prophet, tells his followers about redemption: "The LORD says, 'I will give you back what you lost to the swarming locusts, the hopping locusts, the stripping locusts, and the cutting locusts. . . . and you will praise the LORD your God, who does these miracles for you. . . . Then you will know that I am among my people Israel, that I am the LORD your God, and there is no other.'"[6] If your marriage has lost its vitality, if you have made mistakes, take them to God, and he will redeem them. He walks with you through your marriage. "For the LORD your God is living among you. He is a mighty savior. He will take delight in you with gladness. With his love, he will calm all your fears. He will rejoice over you with joyful songs."[7]

3. He will accept you. God says, "I will claim you as my own people, and I will be your God."[8] When you give yourself to God and ask for his help, you belong to him. He will take care of you. The reality is that the enemy of our marriages and our sex lives—Satan—wants nothing more than for us to live either in Egypt or in the wilderness, alone, isolated, and unaccepted.

But God says that those who call on him for help are not

alone or isolated: "I, yes I, am the one who comforts you. . . . For I am the LORD your God, who stirs up the sea, causing its waves to roar. My name is the LORD of Heaven's Armies. And I have put my words in your mouth and *hidden you safely in my hand.* I stretched out the sky like a canopy and laid the foundations of the earth. I am the one who says to Israel, 'You are my people!'" [9]

The bottom line is that if we are followers of the living God, if we have been freed, redeemed, and accepted, then we need to step out of our frozen states with God and start living as if we are free. That means we put our spouses' needs above our own, we talk to each other about our problems, we seek help, we talk to other Christians, we live confidently.

Many times we forget just how powerful God is. Deep down, we tend to think he's powerless when faced with *our* relationships and sex lives. We forget that nothing is impossible for him—not even healing and strengthening a dead or unsatisfying sex life. Want to know how powerful God is? Want to know the truth about God? Here's what God has to say: "'To whom will you compare me? Who is my equal?' asks the Holy One. Look up into the heavens. Who created all the stars? He brings them out like an army, one after another, calling each by its name. Because of his great power and incomparable strength, not a single one is missing. . . . How can you say the LORD does not see your troubles? . . . How can you say God ignores your rights? Have you never heard? Have you never understood? The LORD is the everlasting God, the Creator of all the earth. He never grows weak or weary. No one can measure the depths of his understanding. He gives power to the weak and strength to the powerless." [10]

Many times we forget just how powerful God is.

That's a pretty awesome, powerful God. But you have to choose to believe and accept his strength, wisdom, and power. You have to let him be God of your life—both outside and *inside* the bedroom.

ASKING GOD FOR HELP

Sometimes husbands and wives suffer needless pain because they place all of their expectations on each other. When a husband feels as if his wife is not meeting his needs, he tends to blame her. When a wife expects her husband to meet all of her needs and he doesn't, she often nurses hurt. The cycle continues, and the pain and resentment grow.

Sometimes husbands and wives suffer needless pain because they place all of their expectations on each other.

"I often felt hurt if my husband, Rod, wasn't sensitive to my needs," Jocelyn confessed. "I felt my needs were justified, so I would badger him or try to manipulate him into meeting them. Or I would blame him, creating more distance between us. If I would talk to him about it, we often ended up arguing, only intensifying the hurt. It was a downward spiral. I often cried myself to sleep.

"Then one day I recognized that I was placing all of the responsibility for meeting my needs on Rod. I began to realize that only God could fill my needs. I thought about some verses in the New Testament: 'Don't worry about anything; instead, pray about everything. Tell God what you need, and thank him for all he has done.'[11] So, when I felt that Rod wasn't meeting my needs, instead of trying to make him change, I followed the instructions in the verse. I talked with God about it, saying something like, 'God, Rod was so distant tonight, and I felt hurt by that. He is so preoccupied by work that I feel like a widow. Please help me. If I am demanding too much, show me that. If I need to let go of my need, help me to do that. Help us to get closer to each other. I forgive him for becoming so absorbed in his work; help him find balance. I give you my need. I trust you to hear me. Thank you that Rod is responsible and faithful.' I tell God what I need. Then I let it go.

"I've begun a discipline of this, and several remarkable things have happened. First, I feel less anxious about my needs. Second, I feel as if somehow I free Rod from needing to be everything to me. Third—and this one takes my breath away—I often find that slowly, over time, Rod changes. One time I was upset because he dismissed how discouraged I was because of a relationship problem I was having with a friend. Several days after I had prayed about it, without my saying anything to him, he came to me while I was at the computer, gave me a shoulder massage, and said, 'How are things between you and Sarah? Have you resolved things? I know how disheartened you were by how she treated you.' We went to the couch, and he listened as I talked about the rift with Sarah. When I cried, he took me in his arms. I never could have orchestrated that. But God knew, and he met my needs through my husband. Later that night Rod and I held each other in bed, and I told him how much I appreciated his sensitivity, how much he had helped me. He told me how much he loved me, and then we made love. Again, I never could have scripted that. But it was wonderful."

FILLING THE VOID

When God created us, he made us to need him. It's as if he created us with a hole in our hearts. Although some of the hole gets filled by our spouses, they can never entirely fill it. Why? Because they weren't meant to. God was.

When we don't allow God to fill us, we become restless. We feel empty and unfulfilled, and we can become brittle. Our culture tries to fill that emptiness with sex, claiming that if you experience more pleasure, you will feel satisfied. But we discover that the thrill of sex lasts only for a while, and then the hollow, empty feeling returns.

Make God part of your daily life, including your sexual relationship. Allow him to fill you.

Unleash the power of heaven so that you can experience heaven on earth. The Garden of Eden in your own bedroom. Why not? You may be thinking, *Yeah, that sounds great, but my spouse and I are nowhere near that kind of experience.* You may struggle to connect spiritually to God or to each other, even though you know you need God's supernatural help to love your spouse over the long haul and to endure the pain when you're hurt.

But God is a God of second chances. He is a God who performs miracles. His forgiveness gives us a second chance, and that includes second chances in the bedroom.

Have you made mistakes you regret? Do you have memories you wish you didn't have? Do you have places in your life or mind or heart where you've hidden secret sin that you don't know what to do with? Are you weighed down by the baggage you think nobody knows about?

Let your sexual mistakes and problems bring you to the place of understanding how powerful forgiveness is. You can meet and experience not only the Creator of sex, but the Creator of grace. Grace is unmerited favor, but God longs to offer it to us.

Many couples say, "Yes, I understand God created sex." But we want you to understand that God is interested in your sex life today, right now. It's okay to pray about your sex life. It's not weird! He really wants us to come to him about *anything*—and that includes our sex lives.

What are the barriers that keep you from inviting God into your marriage? Were you and your spouse taught that you talk about God only on Sundays—that he's not a central part of your life? Or maybe one of you simply isn't interested in spiritual things. Maybe you have secret sin. Maybe you're new Christians and you simply don't know how. Don't let the excuses stop you from having the kind of intimacy God truly desires for you to have in your life and marriage.

REWARDS OF SPIRITUAL INTIMACY

When you pursue a growing, vibrant faith in Jesus Christ, both individually and together as a couple, certain things begin to take place.

God is free to reveal any hurts, emotional baggage, or pain you have and begin to heal your wounded spirit. He often does this when you read the Bible and share its insights together. Spiritual intimacy will allow you to experience transparent honesty, to be able to share fears, anxieties, joys, and dreams.

As you grow spiritually, you will see each other's character become stronger and yet more gentle and loving. Watching that transformation provides a basis for feeling more trust and security in marriage.

As you grow spiritually, you will see each other's character
become stronger and yet more gentle and loving.

Jennie shared her story with us: "My husband and I weren't raised in the same church, so we rarely attended church together. I hated going by myself because I wanted to share this part of my life with my husband. After a while I quit going. I began to feel alone. I knew there had to be more to life. Six years ago, I started listening to God calling me back to him. God led me to a great church, and I began to turn my life around. Although I begged my husband to go to church with me, he wouldn't. I felt as if

God wanted me to focus my attention on my relationship with him, rather than forcing my husband to attend church. After a while my husband saw a change in me as I continued to work on my relationship with Christ. My husband began attending church with me. He listened when God called him, and now he's leading a ministry team at our church. We worship together; we pray together. I now feel as if our family has a higher purpose. God has saved our marriage and our family."

Growing spiritually will also strengthen your sex life. When we counsel couples, we find that couples who are growing in their spiritual lives are also deepening their sex lives. Many people report experiencing deep spiritual satisfaction as a result of their lovemaking. Both sex and spirituality involve intimate parts of our being. Spirituality is not void of passion. When you are filled with adoration, devotion, and respect, you want to share those intense feelings with your spouse. Writing in *Good Housekeeping*, Lisa Collier Cool says, "People who see sex as intercourse only are more likely to talk about boredom, deception, and distance in their relationships. But those who feel a strong spiritual connection with their partner say that as love and trust build over the years, their sexual relationship grows and grows."[12]

One of the things we treasure about our own marriage is seeing each other pursue a spiritual life. Sharing what God is revealing to us through the Bible, prayer, and worship enriches our lives and leads us to a level of intimacy that makes sex a wonderful expression of our oneness. The discipline of pursuing a stronger faith is not foreplay to great sex, but great sex occurs as husbands and wives seek a great God. There is no greater entrée to oneness in sexual intimacy than when husbands and wives prayed about their sex lives and bring clean hearts into the sexual relationship.

In turn, a satisfying sex life can spur a man to pursue a spiritual connection with his wife. The sexual act symbolizes unity. When he experiences the intimacy of a physical connection with his wife, he better understands what spiritual intimacy should look and feel like. Consider what Kevin Leman writes: "The notion of two people becoming one is a profoundly spiritual truth. As a Christian, I believe the sex act has as much to say about what happens within our souls as it does about what goes on inside our bodies. A husband and a wife create a holy union marked by a distinctly spiritual element. A man may have difficulty with contemplative prayer, but this is a spirituality he can truly enjoy!"[13]

The Ultimate Intimacy

Be honest—have you ever thought that prayer would have anything to do with your sex life? Yet, the Bible tells us to "never stop praying."[14] So in essence we pray while we're doing everything: working, gardening, cleaning, relaxing, jogging, driving, shopping, bathing—*and* making love.

If you really think about it, it makes sense to pray about your sex life. After all, if God created sex, the sacredness of it almost demands that you surround it with prayer. Through prayer we come to a realization that ultimately God is in control of every part of our lives, so we are free to release any fear, anxiety, or guilt we may be experiencing.

The two most intimate things a husband and wife can do are have sex and pray. Combine prayer and sex, and you and your spouse move into the most powerful, selfless, guilt-free experience you can have. It's as if the connection you share with your spouse and your Creator makes that time holy. Prayer moves you into the very presence of God.

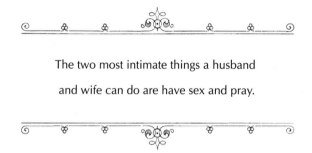

The two most intimate things a husband

and wife can do are have sex and pray.

Research shows that the happiest couples are those who pray together. One study showed that 75 percent of people who pray with their spouses often describe their marriages as "very happy," compared with 57 percent of those who don't.[15] And couples who frequently pray together are twice as likely to describe their marriage as being highly romantic and to report considerably higher sexual satisfaction.[16]

We receive countless e-mails and letters like this one: "My husband, Daryl, and I had been married several years but were struggling. We were miserable in our marriage; I was dealing with depression, and Daryl was just angry all the time. We barely communicated, and our sex life was dead. We're both Christians. We prayed at meals and with our kids before bedtime, but we never prayed together as a couple. Then we hit a wall. I started to suffer from panic attacks. We were so desperate for help that we started to pray together. I never realized how powerful prayer is. I could feel my panic attacks start to subside, and Daryl and I began to talk again. We became intimate again. Since we've been praying together, we've been able to communicate at a more intimate level than ever before. We're more patient with each other. Romance has begun to bloom again, and our 'first love' for each other is once again burning bright. We still have our moments, and sometimes busyness gets in the way, but we have made praying together an everyday commitment. We can't afford not to!"

Many women tell us that they struggle and are disappointed with their husbands' lack of spiritual interest. We have learned that if God is stirring a wife, she can ask God to soften her husband's heart toward spiritual things. And she can ask her husband to read the Bible and pray with her.

We want to give you a thirty-day challenge: For one month pray for your spouse every day at the same time. It could be while you are brushing your teeth, jogging, eating breakfast—whatever works for you. The key is that you pray daily at the same time.

What can you pray about? Pray that your spouse's heart will be open to listening to God's wisdom, insight, and direction. Ask God to show you how to encourage your spouse with creativity. Pray for and about your sex life. Pray that an awesome sense of wonder and love will wash over you and your spouse as you make love. Pray that you will be selfless in your lovemaking. Pray that your mind will be clear to think of nothing but your spouse and the pleasure you both can experience. Thank God for your spouse's body and beauty. Thank God for orgasms! Thank God for those little tingles you feel when you become aroused. Thank him for your spouse's soft breath on your skin, for lips that kiss, for toes that curl during an orgasm.

BUT WHAT IF MY SPOUSE ISN'T INTERESTED IN SPIRITUAL INTIMACY?

Some people struggle to get their spouses interested in spiritual things. If you find yourself in that place, here are some ways you can make spiritual intimacy more appealing.

1. Present your case. Talking to your spouse about spiritual matters may be difficult for you. Counselor David Clarke offers some advice. Tell your spouse you want to discuss something important and ask when would be a good time to talk. Avoid making an emotional argument for your case. Instead, make your approach logical and practical. Your point is not to pressure or appear spiritually superior. Understand that he or she won't respond right away. When you sit down to talk, tell your spouse you don't want him or her to respond now (give your spouse time to process what you will say). Present your case in a straightforward and brief way (keep it to five or ten minutes). Tell your spouse that your marriage is missing something—and you realize it's spiritual intimacy. Then list the benefits: If you spend time together praying, reading the Bible, and attending church, you'll grow spiritually as individuals; you'll create physical and emotional intimacy in your marriage; and you'll receive God's blessing. Ask your spouse to think about what you've said. It's okay if he or she doesn't respond immediately because you've clearly stated the need, established spiritual bonding as a priority, and set the stage for strategy.[17]

2. Focus on your own spiritual life. The Bible teaches that it's possible to win a spouse to Christ without even saying a word.[18] You can draw your spouse to Christ by exhibiting a faith that's authentic. Share your spiritual life with your spouse. Ask if it's okay if you periodically talk about your spiritual life. Share how God is guiding and teaching you. Reveal spiritual triumphs and disappointments. Mention what you're praying for, and share God's answers to your prayers. Don't let your spouse's apparent lack of interest discourage you. Tell your spouse gently and lovingly when you see God working in his or her life. Pick the occasions as God guides, and say only a sentence or two.

3. Look for incremental growth. Don't expect too much too soon. Suggest that you'd like to pray together, and look for an indication that your spouse is open. Then begin by thanking God for your spouse. Keep it brief. Then ask your spouse to pray as well. Affirm whatever growth you see. Above all, don't give up. Imagine how God is working in your spouse's life and how he is preparing to do great things in and through both of you.

When you as a couple work together to grow spiritually, your sex life will also deepen. When you pursue a vital, vibrant relationship with Jesus Christ—individually *and* together—you will experience true oneness, trust, and security. That's the true secret to a great sex life.

CHAPTER 13

Facing the Deeper Issues

This book has attempted to cover the main sexual issues that most couples deal with in their marriages. However, some couples struggle with deeper issues: unhealthy fantasies, lust, infidelity, date rape, memories of previous sexual encounters, exposure to pornographic Web sites, or childhood sexual abuse. All of these can have devastating effects on a marriage. And yet, because as Christ-followers we serve a God who is bigger than any struggle or problem, we know that even in the midst of all these challenges, we have hope that true sexual intimacy *can* occur.

Even though we will address some of these deeper issues in the following pages, we realize that we cannot cover them with the depth and completeness they really demand. If you find yourself struggling with any of these issues, use the sections of this chapter as a starting place. Then get professional help from a Christian sex therapist. We know many couples cringe at the thought of seeking counseling from a sex therapist, but it's important to remember that getting trustworthy help is nothing to be ashamed of. You are taking proactive steps to build a strong foundation for your sex life and marriage. That's courageous and honorable. Keep pursuing the right path. You will find help, hope, and healing there.

FACING THE ISSUES TOGETHER

Many times an injured spouse will withdraw and think, *It's* my *problem. I will handle it.* A problem with a sexual issue is never just one spouse's problem; it's a *couple's* problem. It's not *I* have a problem; it's *we* have a problem. You need to talk about it *together.* You need to make a plan *together.* You need to decide *together* what kind of outside help is needed.

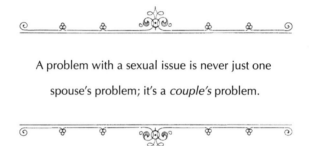

A problem with a sexual issue is never just one

spouse's problem; it's a *couple's* problem.

There is no room for isolation. When couples get married, it's easy for them to forget that the primary goal of marriage is not their own personal fulfillment; the goal of marriage is oneness. The goal is to reflect God's love and wisdom. Fulfillment is the joyful by-product of sharing in his goodness. Whatever the problem, promise each other that you will handle it *together.*

When you understand these deeper issues and take them to God, you can begin to release them. But if they remain secrets and private memories, Satan can use them as destructive tools. The enemy of our holiness and purity delights in drawing us into the shadows of temptation or memories or pain of the past. Whenever Satan can keep us from focusing on our growth in Christ or from pursuing godliness in our marriages, he gets a foothold that begins to erode the sanctity of the marriage and leads to the destruction of oneness. Don't let that happen to your marriage and sex life. Commit together to protect your relationship with the supernatural help of God. If you ask, he will help you.

The next several sections of the chapter will explore the impact of four major problem areas: premarital sex, pornography, infidelity, and sexual trauma. In our experience with thousands of couples, we have seen many who have been devastated by these issues. But we've also talked with countless couples whom God has redeemed and whose marriages have become whole again. Our prayer is that you will experience that same wholeness.

Intimacy Overrated: Premarital Sex

We guess that many people reading this book had sex before marriage—either with the person who eventually became their spouse or with some other person. From the experience we've had with thousands of couples, we can also guess that if you had premarital sex, you probably have had or are having sexual problems as a result of that activity.

What's the big deal about sleeping with someone outside of marriage? When you have sex outside the boundary of marriage, you give a part of yourself to that other person. And the part that you give is sanctified—set apart—specifically for your *spouse*. Sex outside marriage often causes couples to lose the innocence and anticipation of true sexual fulfillment. But it also sets up opportunities for comparisons and memories of previous lovers or experiences. Many couples have no idea that some of the sexual issues they currently have go back to what each of them did sexually before marriage.

A number of years ago a young married woman shared with us that she had been sexually active in college, and the memories kept resurfacing to haunt her. And now she is struggling sexually with her husband because sex takes her back to what she did with her old college boyfriend. The consequences of her choice have robbed her *and* her husband of the freedom they should be able to experience together.

Why are there consequences to premarital sex? Because sex is not just an act. It's spiritual. Sex connects not only two bodies but also two souls, melding them into one. We've had people tell us, "Yeah, but that was twenty years ago." We tell them, "It doesn't matter how long ago it was." Every time you have sex with a person, you bond and tie your souls together, whether or not you intend to.

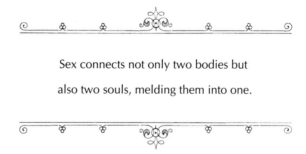

Sex connects not only two bodies but
also two souls, melding them into one.

In her book *Inviting God to Your Wedding*, Martha Williamson says, "Someone once described it to me this way: When you . . . are intimate with someone—it's like gluing two pieces of wood together. When you finally pull the wood apart, it doesn't come off clean. Each takes a little piece of the other away with it. The more relationships you have and the more sex you have, the more pieces of other people you are carrying around with you. And unfortunately, by the time you get married, the joy of sex and the thrill of discovery can be significantly diminished."[1]

You may be thinking, *Yeah, I slept with someone outside of marriage. I regret doing it because the relationship didn't work out, but I don't feel as if I gave a part of my soul. I don't feel like anything happened.*

We always tell people, "The earth revolves around the sun. We don't feel that either, but that doesn't mean it doesn't happen." Your premarital sexual activity—together or with others—will have an impact on your current sexual health and joy.

Many people who have premarital sex later struggle with guilt and shame. Another destructive by-product of premarital sex is that a spouse compares marital sex with the premarital experience. Some people find premarital sex exciting merely because it is forbidden. They like the thrill of the illicit nature of it. But married sex is different. It is satisfying because it is exclusive and safe. When married couples entertain memories of former sexual incidents, they experience a disconnect. They tend to romanticize the past. When they begin comparing a spouse to a premarital sexual partner, they don't see the truth. It's a faulty sense of comparison.

Finding Help: Intimacy Retraced

The good news is that you can retrace your steps and find deep intimacy with your spouse. If you had sex before you were married, the first thing to do is to understand that you and/or your spouse stepped out of God's will for your marriage. You can recapture the joy of your marriage by making it right with God. Confess to each other and to God. Seek forgiveness from both your spouse and God. Then forgive yourself. Let yourself off the hook. If your spouse was the one who had sex before marriage, then forgive him or her for giving away something that belonged only to you. Forgive your spouse for cheating you out of what was meant to be pure and fun and a discovery.

You can recapture the joy of your
marriage by making it right with God.

Also affirm what is pleasurable to you. You've looked in the rearview mirror of promiscuity. You've prayed for release from that. Now it's important to receive affirmation from each other, to build a firm foundation of sexual unity for your marriage. In essence you are reclaiming your moral and sexual purity; you are breaking those soul ties that happened outside of marriage.

Martha Williamson talks about how she and her husband broke the soul ties that formed during their promiscuous relationships. They wrote a list of all their past relationships, both sexual and emotional. "I had names to put on my list and so did Jon," she writes in *Inviting God to Your Wedding*. "We approached this with complete honesty. As I wrote, I could feel how much I wanted back all the pieces of myself that I had left glued to other people. And how much I wanted to be rid of the pieces that were still glued to me." She writes that after they had completed their inventories, "We supported each other in prayer as we brought each name on our lists before the Lord. We asked God to forgive us, and we committed ourselves to turn away from our past relationships and past behaviors. One by one, we crossed the names off. Finally, we ripped up our lists, threw the pieces on the floor, and said good-bye to our past forever, acknowledging that it no longer had any power over us.

"Suddenly I felt healed and whole again, free of the pieces of other people that I had been carrying around. And all the pieces of myself that I had given away were gathered and returned to me. I hadn't felt like that in years. I felt cleansed. . . . I looked at [Jon] and smiled. He was now truly my one and only. And I was truly his."[2]

When you confess and forgive yourself and each other, God will begin to quiet the memories. He will replace the old memories with new ones.

INTIMACY STOLEN: PORNOGRAPHY

A friend who is a divorce attorney told us that one of the primary reasons that people divorce is the impact of pornography. And it's not just men who are addicted. More and more women are becoming visually stimulated and addicted to Internet pornography.

In the past a person had to go to the store to buy a *Playboy*. Now people can view pornography in the privacy of their offices or homes by clicking on the Internet. At a recent conference one man told us, "It used to be that you had to chase after your sin. Now your sin chases after you."

What's truly unfortunate is that we know of Christian counselors who encourage or suggest that their clients use pornography to spice things up in the bedroom.

Whether your spouse enjoys pornography or whether you both view pornography as a way to make sex sizzle, the result is the same: Pornography damages your sex life and marriage. Friends, pornography is serious sin. There is nothing God-honoring or spouse-honoring about using porn. Nothing. Ever.

Why? We can think of several reasons:

1. Pornography introduces a third party into your bedroom. Pornography contaminates and desecrates the holiness, purity, and sanctity of marriage. By bringing photos of others' bodies into your sex life, it is as if you are committing an act of adultery. The Bible tells us, "Marriage should be honored by all, and the marriage bed kept pure, for God will judge the adulterer and all the sexually immoral."[3]

2. Pornography introduces comparison into your sex life. You and your spouse can never measure up to the airbrushed, enhanced, sex-hungry bodies you see on porn sites. Pornography only leads to dissatisfaction and false expectations of yourself and your spouse.

3. Pornography is completely devoid of what we were made for—relationship. Even though viewing pornography and masturbating bring sexual release, they leave a person empty and unfulfilled. We know of one young man who sought help for his addiction when his marriage failed. He told us, "I did it because I didn't have to make any kind of relationship commitment. My wife was too much work, and this was fast and easy and accessible. And I got my needs taken care of. But at what price? It's cost me my marriage."

4. Pornography is like a drug. The more you view pornography, the more you need in order to become aroused. It creates a tolerance level that goes higher and higher. What you once viewed begins not to have the same effect, so you need to up the ante in order to bring about the stimulation.

FINDING HELP: INTIMACY RESTORED

David Goetz, author of *Death by Suburb*, tells the story of how Garrison Keillor, the humorist and author of the popular *Lake Wobegon*, wrote an advice column for Salon.com. One woman asked what she should do about her husband's two-hundred-dollar-a-month pornography habit. Keillor's advice was for her to tell him that she would like to participate too, but that two hundred dollars a month was too much, so she'd like him to shop around for better deals. "In his dry, sardonic way," Goetz says, "Keillor was attempting, I think, to push her to whack him back to reality and fidelity. Why masturbate to digital images of animal-like sex when you can make love to real flesh and blood?"[4] If you or your spouse is viewing pornography, here are some steps to take:

1. Face the truth. The first thing is to face the truth of what pornography is. "All that glitters is not gold," as the cliché goes. Face the reality that pornography cannot coexist with a healthy, God-honoring, vibrant, successful sex life.

2. Establish boundaries. Tell each other when you are tempted by pornography, and hold each other accountable. Allow others to hold you accountable too. Be vigilant and intentional about keeping boundaries in place.

Sam and Ginny know about boundaries and accountability. Ginny told us, "Sam doesn't spend a lot of time on the Internet. He gets on, does what he needs to do, and signs off. Several weeks ago he said to me, 'I have to tell you something. I can't believe this happened, but I just want to tell you.' He explained that as he was checking a work-related Web site, all of a sudden an XXX-rated Web site popped up. As he was talking about the temptation and how he resisted it, I was thinking, *Why is he telling me this? He didn't have to do that. I would never have known.* But by telling me, Sam was letting me know that he isn't going to fall to temptation. Sam's honesty strengthened my ability to trust him. He didn't have to tell me; he didn't gain anything by it. But in another sense he gained the world by it."

Setting boundaries means placing the computer in a heavily trafficked area in the house—the kitchen or family room. It means putting a filter on the computer. We've heard of filters that will send e-mails to three different "accountability" people if someone tries to access a pornographic Web site. It means you go to bed together at night. It means doing research before you watch certain movies—and being willing to walk out of a movie that is even mildly pornographic.

3. Take it slowly. It's naïve to think, *I'll go to Victoria's Secret, buy a new teddy, and everything will be okay. If I do this, it will stop my husband's addiction.* Take one step at a time. The important thing is to replace the old visuals with the new. Every time you focus on making love to each other, focusing only on each other, you rewire the old memories. And while you're doing that and reintroducing the healthy, real intimacy of marriage, you are diminishing the other.

4. Realize that healing takes time. When a spouse relapses, stay in the game with him or her. Offering criticism will not help. Pray for him or her. Go to counseling together. Love your spouse. Respond rationally with, "Let's think this through calmly," rather than responding out of pain or emotion. Otherwise, the person will shut down, deny it, and withdraw—all things that impede healing and hinder sexual intimacy.

How do you confront your spouse rationally, without the emotion? If you suspect that your spouse is viewing Internet pornography, check the Internet history. Then print it out, and simply—without a word—place it in front of him or her. Try that every week. And if there's nothing there, print that out, place it in front of your spouse, and affirm him or her.

5. Guard your eyes. Guarding your eyes means looking away, bouncing your eyes to some other object, physically getting up and going somewhere else, such as to the kitchen for a cup of coffee. Celeste mentioned to us, "During the winter months, Joel and I get our exercise by walking in an indoor mall. It always impresses me that he looks away as we walk past Victoria's Secret. It's not that he is a prude. It's not that he doesn't appreciate sexy lingerie; I know that from personal experience. But Joel knows the power of visual stimulation, and the nearly nude mannequins and the seductive posters in the display windows can tempt him. When he turns his eyes away, I feel secure. I respect him so much for that."

When you starve your eyes and eliminate the junk food from your life, you'll deeply crave "real food"—the wife whom God provided for you. Listen to what happened to Fred Stoeker, one of the authors of *Every Man's Battle: Winning the War on Sexual Temptation,* when he committed himself to getting rid of the visual junk food:

> After I'd gone cold turkey on sexual images for about three weeks, I remember vividly how Brenda noticed the geometric rise in my desire for her. Constantly telling her how beautiful she looked, I was all over her, patting her, hugging her, touching her. I also was desiring intercourse far more often, and as the new higher pace continued, it dawned upon Brenda that this might not be just some simple jag or a phase. She panicked, blurting out, "What am I doing to make myself so attractive? I have to stop it!"
>
> That moment was hilarious. I told her what was going on and that I couldn't really help my heightened desire for her. "All my desires are coming straight at you, and I don't quite know what to do about it yet. I promise I'll work hard to get back to an equilibrium that we both can live with." Brenda didn't know whether to be relieved or shocked, but she expressed a willingness to allow me time to find that equilibrium—and to put up with me until then. Those days revealed to me just how much I'd been stealing from Brenda.[5]

INTIMACY VIOLATED: INFIDELITY

It seems as if infidelity is an epidemic these days. According to the *Los Angeles Times* article "The Roots of Temptation," one in five people is likely to cheat on a spouse.[6] The zinger is that many people who report being in happy marriages commit adultery. Like everyone else, married men and women have an appetite for flirtation and sexually charged attention. Studies show their need for connection warps their judgment, even when they fully appreciate the risks of infidelity. Most affairs don't occur because of sexual problems at home—they happen because of disconnects in the marriage. Although the responsibility for an affair always lies with the person violating the marriage vows, the other spouse often contributes to the breakdown of the connection.

Most affairs don't occur because of sexual problems at home—

they happen because of disconnects in the marriage.

Noted marriage researcher John Gottman says, "It's not uncommon for someone to cheat and then blame their partner for it. If someone is lonely or feels their mate has lost all interest in them, they can rationalize that they were driven to have an affair."[7] Researcher Debbie Layton-Tholl has found that most people don't pursue adulterous relationships because they want new sexual partners. Of the 4,300 respondents who completed her questionnaire, more than 90 percent reported that only after there had been a lack of intimacy and a loss of emotional and sexual satisfaction did the dissatisfied partner look for a new lover to fulfill his or her needs.[8]

But infidelity can bring unbearable pain. When emotional and physical affairs happen, it is not only a betrayal but also a deep brokenness. The pain may be so intense that it's hard not to keep reliving the experience. The offended spouse may keep bringing it up, and the offender may get frustrated and say, "I said I was sorry. I asked for forgiveness. Why can't you get over this so we can move on?" Restoration isn't easy. An affair is a *major* breakdown of commitment. It may happen only one time, in a quick tryst, but it takes years to rebuild the trust that is lost. Restoration calls for a lot of patience, a lot of contrition, a lot of love.

If one of you has been unfaithful in your marriage, you both need to ask some questions. The unfaithful spouse needs to ask, What will I do to prevent another affair? The betrayed spouse needs to ask, Am I committed to restoring this marriage? Scripture does say that in the case of adultery, God allows divorce.[9] But if you are committed to restoration, then we can give you a plan.

First, confess your sin and mistakes to each other. Then ask God to help you forgive each other. Next, reestablish and reaffirm your commitment. Without commitment, you will be doing restoration work without a safety net.

An initial conversation about commitment and restoration might sound something like this: "Sharon, you committed adultery. Your infidelity has come to the surface, but I want you to know that I want to make this marriage work. I'm committed to you and to our marriage. I'm going to stand under God's promise that redemption and forgiveness and grace can occur. I have to confess that sometimes I don't feel like trying to make it work. It doesn't make sense to me; it's counterintuitive. But I am more committed to you than I am to holding on to this offense. I'm committing myself to restoration partly because of the kids. Part of me wants to do it because my parents were divorced, and I don't want to repeat that. I want to break that cycle. Another part of me wants to do it because I believe that I didn't meet all of your needs either. So even though I didn't cheat on you, I cheated you. I have to tell you that I'm really scared. But I want to reaffirm that I love Jesus and I believe that the work God is doing in you can bear fruit."

This husband expresses not only his vulnerability but also his commitment. He is relying on God to work in both his wife and himself.

Another woman told us that after she learned of her husband's infidelity, she committed herself to restoration, but not because she necessarily trusted her husband. She told him, "I'm not sure I trust you, but I trust God. And I trust the work he's doing. So I want to reaffirm my commitment to working on this marriage." That's the place to start.

As you work toward restoration, you will grieve, you will weep, you will blame, you will fight. You may come through each day bloody, but stay the course.

FINDING HELP: INTIMACY REDEEMED

The big issue is learning to rebuild the trust. What can you do to help your spouse begin to trust you again? Here are a few steps to take.

1. Cut off all contact with the third person. If that means leaving your job, quitting the church choir, or dropping the karate class so that you do not have contact with the other person, then do it. This is serious business.

2. Report any contact you do have. If you do have contact with the other person, report it to your spouse, regardless of who initiated it. The offended spouse needs to have zero tolerance about your contact with the other person. If you end up confiding in him or her again, you only create another injury, another secret, another potential affair.

3. Make yourself accountable. Your spouse will be watching to make sure you are true to your word. If you say you're going to be home in five minutes but you see that you're going to be late, call and say why you are not home. The smallest thing will set off your spouse and begin the destructive cycle of mistrust and suspicion. You may feel like an adolescent to have to report your activities, but for the first several months it's an important step in rebuilding trust.

4. List all your questions, then take the list to a professional biblical counselor or sex therapist. If you are the offended spouse, write out every question you have. No question is off-limits. Your questions may include,

- How did you meet him/her?
- Where were you when you had sex?
- Where was I?
- Did you tell him/her that you love him/her?
- What did he/she wear?
- How many times did you meet?
- How many times did you have sex?
- What did he/she do for you that I didn't do?
- What lies did you tell me to cover up your activity?

The point is to purge. Write out the scariest issues you need to get out. We've seen spouses' lists run twenty to thirty pages, with hundreds of questions.

When you have completed your list, take it to a counselor, who can help you sort it out and discern which questions to ask the offending spouse.

5. Confront your spouse with the condensed list. This is best done in the presence of a counselor who can help you navigate through this delicate issue. Try to ask the questions as calmly and rationally as you can. If you were the spouse who had the affair, answer your spouse's questions with enough information so that he or she can be at peace with moving past it but with so much specificity that it is too overwhelming. The bottom line is to make sure you confess everything. Everything. When you hold back, Satan uses those unconfessed secrets to bring destruction to your marriage. When we counsel couples in this situation, we often review the questions with the offending spouse and filter the report to the offended spouse with his or her permission and blessing. The wounded spouse should not need to carry the burden of knowing excessive details about the offenses.

6. Forgive. It's essential to understand that forgiveness isn't a onetime deal. Many times when the pain resurfaces, you need to choose to forgive again and let it go. In her book *Avoiding the Greener Grass Syndrome*, Nancy Anderson writes about how she learned forgiveness from her father. Here's what he told Nancy and her husband, Ron, after her affair had been discovered:

When you tell someone you're sorry, it's very different from asking for their forgiveness. Your "sorry-ness" is *your* decision. But when you ask someone to forgive you, that's *their* decision. That's why people avoid asking forgiveness. It gives all the power to the other person. . . .

Ron, when you forgive someone, you make a choice . . . to banish the offense from your mind and your heart. Jesus said that after he forgives us, our sins are as far away as the East is from the West. In other words, they're pardoned. Not because we're *not* guilty, but because we *are*. Our pardon is undeserved. . . . It's a gift to us from God. If you decide to pardon Nancy's sin against you, you can never use it as a weapon against her. And if you do make the choice to forgive her, God will give you the strength to start a new life together. But if you don't want to forgive her . . . if you want to hold on to the pain, and punish her, and keep her wound open, . . . that will be your choice. But I don't think you'll stay married.[10]

7. Validate the wounded spouse and give restoration some time. When we have been hurt and rejected, we tend to move into self-protection mode, which includes withdrawal, stonewalling, being distant and cold, and lashing out to punish the offender for the pain.

If you are the offender, remember that your actions have seriously damaged your spouse's ability to trust you. It's very important for you to validate your spouse. Tell him or her of your love, and show it in actions that build trust. Call home, and stay accountable if you are late or need to run errands.

Then be patient. You will want your spouse to get over it and move back to where you were before he or she learned of your affair. But it's not that simple. Your spouse needs to get out the toxic waste of your actions. Only then can you begin to move in the direction of restoration. Through intense counseling and a good support system, you will come to a point when your spouse will let it go. But that will take time and help.

8. Reintroduce sex slowly. Again, if you are the offending spouse, don't assume that once you and your spouse have talked about the affair you can resume a normal sex life. Restoring intimacy after an affair is a process. First, make sure you see a physician so you're not transmitting disease. But for a while, most likely, you and your spouse will take a vacation from sex. Always, the offended spouse is the one who sets the pace for lovemaking because sex after an affair has an emotional and spiritual rawness to it that requires willingness and grace. But is it possible to restore that sexual relationship so that it is wonderful? Yes. It takes a lot of time and patience, but it can happen.

Your spouse may forgive you, but that doesn't remove the consequences. And the number one consequence is you're likely not going to get sex for a period of time. When you begin to reintroduce sex, be very patient and gentle. Your spouse will probably not have a lot of resiliency.

9. Act "as if." Even when the ache is there, if you are committed, then act "as if" you love your spouse. Acting "as if" is different from putting on an act. Acting "as if" means that you act in a way that expresses belief that someday you will feel loving again. There is hope in acting "as if." You speak belief to yourself until you *do* believe.

10. Work on the relationship. Work on reconnecting in the areas that need the most attention. Start dating and courting each other again. Don't allow the setbacks to set you back. Once you begin to reconnect emotionally and spiritually, through forgiveness and hard work, the sexual expression will begin to follow.

When Gary was young, his sister had polio. The doctors said she would never walk again, but his dad refused to accept that prediction. His dad said, "Oh, she will walk again. You just wait!" He brought parallel bars into their living room. He put a swimming pool in the backyard. For five years Gary's family focused on making sure that his sister would walk again. And his sister walks today.

It's the same thing with a marriage that has been devastated by infidelity. The couples who make it through successfully have a wartime mentality. They are committed to going *through* the pain, not around it.

11. Pray. Pray and recommit your marriage. Ask God to heal both of you. Stand at your bed, and pray over it. Pray for purity and restoration in your marriage. Pray for protection, that neither you nor your spouse will be tempted again in this area, that you will be strong enough to fight off temptations.

12. Depend on God. In our more than twenty-five years of counseling, we've seen that the couples who have the greatest chance of coming through the effects of infidelity are those with a strong faith in Christ. Plug into a support group at church. Pray, grow spiritually together, keep a journal of your insights and commitments. Cry out to God. His Holy Spirit can heal places of the heart that we, in our humanness, cannot touch. Do you trust the work that God is doing in your spouse? Restoration is teamwork: you, your spouse, God, your local church's support system, and a biblical counselor. And somehow God will knit together your hearts so that you can celebrate the gift he's given you.

INTIMACY DAMAGED: SEXUAL TRAUMA

In an article about her own healing from the effects of childhood sexual abuse on her marriage, Mary DeMuth reports these statistics: "According to the Department of Justice, by age 18, one in four women and one in six men have been sexually abused. What happens to the titanic number of sexually abused men and women when they marry and enter regular sexual experiences with their mates? One study published in *Contemporary Family Therapy* estimates that 56 percent of women who were sexually abused as children feel discomfort during sex and 36 percent seek some sort of sexual therapy."[11]

Gary has counseled hundreds of courageous men and women who seek the healing God desires for them. During these intense counseling sessions, he often recommends that they take a "vacation from sex" for a while. He encourages spouses to be extremely intentional about the healing, with the belief that God can restore healthy sexual interests as the restoration occurs. He suggests that couples read Dan Allender's *The Wounded Heart* as they go through counseling to help them understand the issues of shame, guilt, and healing. The biggest mistake is to give up on the potential for a healthy sexual relationship and shut down, compartmentalize sex, or not connect deeply to your spouse.

In her book *Breaking Free*, Beth Moore, who also dealt with childhood abuse, discusses the importance of renewing your mind. She compares it to going through a room, stripping the wallpaper, and repapering it completely. She suggests that you walk through the room of your mind and challenge the lies from Satan, strip them down, and replace them with truth. She suggests you take Scripture passages based on the truth of who you are in God's eyes and put them in your purse or your wallet. When you are out doing errands or waiting in line somewhere, take out the verses and memorize them. Realize that you are rewiring your mind to replace the enemy's messages with God's messages of truth.

It's critical to understand that overcoming the trauma of sexual abuse is a battlefield of the mind. Too often people who have experienced trauma try to repress the pain. Their bodies go through the motions, but the people don't experience wholeness from the inside out. Wholeness is not going to happen right off. But if you just keep taking the next step, healing can come.

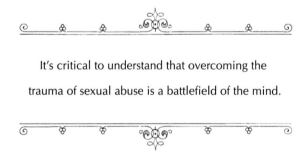

It's critical to understand that overcoming the trauma of sexual abuse is a battlefield of the mind.

Abuse is abuse is abuse—spiritual abuse, emotional abuse, physical abuse, and certainly sexual abuse. All abuse damages the soul, heart, and body. Obviously each kind of abuse has its own uniqueness.

If your spouse has suffered abuse, listen patiently as he or she processes feelings, memories, and fears. Be sensitive to your spouse's needs. An abused spouse will often experience feelings of mistrust toward the other spouse—especially if he or she was molested as a child. As a result of the trauma, your spouse may distrust your touch or become incredibly closed—especially where sex is concerned.

People who have been sexually abused will see sex as wrong, dirty, and shameful. They feel that if they enjoy sex, they are condoning what their abusers did to them. And if they don't enjoy sex, they are a bad spouse. So they become paralyzed. They're frozen and scared, and they may unknowingly disconnect from their marriage relationships.

If you are a victim of sexual abuse, it is important that you get help from somebody who is trained in that area. We encourage you to see a trained Christian sex therapist. And your spouse can join you in therapy later in the process, to learn how to comfort, encourage, and connect.

When Gary coaches a man whose spouse has been abused, he tells him that he can be an incredibly strong instrument God can use to restore his wife's sense of self and her sense of becoming the woman God desires. And often that means the most loving thing a spouse can do is to abstain from sex for a time to allow the hurt spouse to peel back the layers of pain and work through them, to give that spouse a safe place to grieve the loss of innocence and purity. Anybody who's been through this experience has the right to feel loss and pain.

If you suspect your spouse has been sexually abused but she or he doesn't talk about it, it's okay to ask. Be gentle. Some abused men and women have never spoken to anyone else about the abuse, so it may not be easy at first for them to admit it or talk about it.

Jake and Marla's sex life had suffered from the time they were first married. Jake rarely felt as if Marla was completely present for him. And she never liked to kiss or touch him. He began to suspect that maybe she'd been molested as a child. So one evening, he very gently asked her if she had ever been betrayed by anyone. As they began to talk, she finally admitted the horror of what had happened to her. "I feel so ashamed," Marla told him. "I've been wanting to tell you, but I was afraid you wouldn't want me anymore. So it just never seemed to make sense to tell you. And then after we got married, I didn't want to tell you because I thought you'd become angry at me." Jake comforted and affirmed her that night, and they agreed to seek counseling.

FINDING HELP: INTIMACY HEALED

It's important for injured spouses, especially if it they are scarred by childhood sexual abuse, to recognize that they were victims. It wasn't their fault. They are never responsible for what happened to them. It's also important for them to know you love them unconditionally and that you are committed to them and the marriage. Start with these steps:

1. **Recommit to each other.** Remind your bruised spouse that you are not going anywhere, that you accept and love him or her completely, unconditionally. Keep saying that you are in this together—all the way to healing. Tell your spouse you will not wound him or her.

2. Take a break from sex. Tell your spouse that during this season of counseling, until he or she feels more comfortable, you will wait to have sex. It's not enough just to acknowledge the wound. You need to be willing to work with him or her, and that may mean putting aside your own sexual needs—otherwise sex can wound again. We've heard spouses say, "Well, just have sex, and you'll be okay." We disagree. What will probably happen is that the wounded person will merely withdraw and shut down.

3. Seek help as soon as possible. Recovering from sexual abuse requires the help of someone trained to walk with you. Even though friends or Bible study leaders can listen and encourage you, they are not trained in the complexities of the effects of sexual abuse. Find a Christian trauma specialist or sex therapist who is trained to deal with sexual assault.

4. Comfort. Show affection, hold each other, and pray with each other. Mia told us that sometimes while she and her husband were in the middle of sex, she would have a flashback from when she was date-raped. She would freeze and shut down. During those times her husband would hold her and whisper over and over in her ear, "I'm your husband. I love you. I would never hurt you. I'm not the person who raped you. You are safe. Look into my eyes. I am yours. You are mine. We belong to Jesus. We will get through this *together*."

5. Understand that healing takes time. There are no quick fixes for sexual trauma. Many times the victim may feel used or have a distorted view of sex. Healing takes reassurance, listening, and speaking words of comfort and affirmation. Recovering from sexual trauma is a delicate process, and it's important not to impose a timetable on your spouse.

6. Talk about your sexual relationship. In her story about recovering from sexual abuse, Mary DeMuth writes,

> As difficult as it might be, Patrick and I had to speak frankly about our sexual relationship. Through God's strength, I was finally able to tell Patrick, "When you complain about our sexual frequency, I want to give up and never try," or "When you say or do that, I feel used, that I'm only an object."
>
> In that same God-strength, Patrick was able to say, "When you don't place sex and affection as a priority, I don't feel loved," or "When you don't kiss me, I feel distant from you."
>
> We also had to resolve not to hide our anger or pain. Patrick buried his anger over my lack of response and then quit communicating altogether. I erroneously thought if I hid my pain over my past, I could magically improve sexually. But we realized not addressing the truth was disastrous for our sexual relationship.[12]

7. Pray for your spouse. Ask the Holy Spirit to erase the haunting memories, to pour healing oil on your spouse's heart and soul. Remind your spouse of Christ's words of invitation: "Come to me, all of you who are weary and carry heavy burdens, and I will give you rest."[13] Your spouse will take great comfort and strength in knowing that you are praying for him or her. Be God's instrument of healing and rest.

Pray that someday your spouse would be able to say, "I can rejoice in my sufferings because I know that suffering produces perseverance, and perseverance produces character, and character leads to hope. And hope will not disappoint me."[14] Pray that God would remind your spouse that what Satan meant for evil, God can use for good.

A Final Word

We hope this book has helped you grow in understanding not only your own sex needs but also your spouse's needs. Our prayer is that the stories and suggestions in this book will equip and inspire you to meet your spouse's needs more lovingly and fully.

Marriage is a precious gift from God, and sex as part of your marriage relationship is his idea. When we experience sex the way he intends it to be expressed, it knits us together with our spouses in ways that words cannot describe. Becoming one with a spouse through sex is a profound mystery.

We ask you to renew your commitment to love your spouse completely. Enjoy the differences in your maleness and femaleness. Practice serving love, and determine to meet your husband's or wife's needs before your own. Put away selfishness and serve your spouse. God honors that kind of commitment.

We also hope that this book has given you lots of suggestions for how you can deepen the physical, emotional, and spiritual aspects of your sexual relationship. Good sex in a marriage can be fun. Keep the spark alive. Good sex in a marriage can be comforting. Draw your spouse in to the safety of the physical union. Good sex in a marriage honors God. Keep him at the center of your relationship.

We pray that God will bless you with great sex—and a great marriage!

APPENDIX A

WHAT DOES THE BIBLE SAY ABOUT MARRIAGE AND SEX?

The Bible speaks often about the marriage relationship and about sex.
Read through these Scripture passages, and allow them to guide you
and shape your marriage.

God's Intentions for Marriage

God looked over all he had made, and he saw that it was very good!
GENESIS 1:31

Then the LORD God said, "It is not good for the man to be alone. I will
make a helper who is just right for him." GENESIS 2:18

"At last!" the man exclaimed. "This one is bone from my bone, and flesh
from my flesh! . . ." This explains why a man leaves his father and mother
and is joined to his wife, and the two are united into one. Now the man
and his wife were both naked, but they felt no shame. GENESIS 2:23-25

New Testament Thoughts about Marriage

The husband should fulfill his wife's sexual needs, and the wife should
fulfill her husband's needs. 1 CORINTHIANS 7:3

Do not deprive each other of sexual relations, unless you both agree to
refrain from sexual intimacy for a limited time so you can give yourselves
more completely to prayer. Afterward, you should come together again so
that Satan won't be able to tempt you because of your lack of self-control.
1 CORINTHIANS 7:5

Among the Lord's people, women are not independent of men, and men
are not independent of women. For although the first woman came from
man, every other man was born from a woman, and everything comes
from God. 1 CORINTHIANS 11:11-12

A husband is the head of his wife as Christ is the head of the church. He is
the Savior of his body, the church. As the church submits to Christ, so you

wives should submit to your husbands in everything. For husbands, this means love your wives, just as Christ loved the church. He gave up his life for her. . . . As the Scriptures say, "A man leaves his father and mother and is joined to his wife, and the two are united into one." This is a great mystery, but it is an illustration of the way Christ and the church are one. So again I say, each man must love his wife as he loves himself, and the wife must respect her husband. EPHESIANS 5:23-25, 31-33

In the same way, you wives must accept the authority of your husbands. Then, even if some refuse to obey the Good News, your godly lives will speak to them without any words. They will be won over by observing your pure and reverent lives. 1 PETER 3:1-2

Warnings about Behavior in Marriage

You must not commit adultery. EXODUS 20:14

I made a covenant with my eyes not to look with lust at a young woman. JOB 31:1

Drink water from your own well—share your love only with your wife. Why spill the water of your springs in the streets, having sex with just anyone? You should reserve it for yourselves. Never share it with strangers. Let your wife be a fountain of blessing for you. Rejoice in the wife of your youth. She is a loving deer, a graceful doe. Let her breasts satisfy you always. May you always be captivated by her love. Why be captivated, my son, by an immoral woman, or fondle the breasts of a promiscuous woman? For the Lord sees clearly what a man does, examining every path he takes. PROVERBS 5:15-21

Anyone who even looks at a woman with lust has already committed adultery with her in his heart. MATTHEW 5:28

Don't copy the behavior and customs of this world, but let God transform you into a new person by changing the way you think. ROMANS 12:2

Don't you realize that all of you together are the temple of God and that the Spirit of God lives in you? God will destroy anyone who destroys this temple. For God's temple is holy, and you are that temple. 1 CORINTHIANS 3:16-17

Run from sexual sin! No other sin so clearly affects the body as this one does. For sexual immorality is a sin against your own body. Don't you realize that your body is the temple of the Holy Spirit, who lives in you and was given to you by God? You do not belong to yourself, for God bought you with a high price. So you must honor God with your body. 1 CORINTHIANS 6:18-20

Give honor to marriage, and remain faithful to one another in marriage. God will surely judge people who are immoral and those who commit adultery. HEBREWS 13:4

Guidelines for Healthy Relationships

Some people make cutting remarks, but the words of the wise bring healing. PROVERBS 12:18

Awake, north wind! Rise up, south wind! Blow on my garden and spread its fragrance all around. Come into your garden, my love; taste its finest fruits. . . . I am my lover's, and my lover is mine. He browses among the lilies. . . . I am my lover's, and he claims me as his own. SONG OF SONGS 4:16; 6:3; 7:10

Love is patient and kind. Love is not jealous or boastful or proud or rude. It does not demand its own way. It is not irritable, and it keeps no record of being wronged. It does not rejoice about injustice but rejoices whenever the truth wins out. Love never gives up, never loses faith, is always hopeful, and endures through every circumstance. 1 CORINTHIANS 13:4-7

Anyone who belongs to Christ has become a new person. The old life is gone; a new life has begun! 2 CORINTHIANS 5:17

Let no corrupt communication proceed out of your mouth, but that which is good to the use of edifying, that it may minister grace unto the hearers. EPHESIANS 4:29, KJV

Get rid of all bitterness, rage, anger, harsh words, and slander, as well as all types of evil behavior. Instead, be kind to each other, tenderhearted, forgiving one another, just as God through Christ has forgiven you. EPHESIANS 4:31-32

Don't be selfish; don't try to impress others. Be humble, thinking of others as better than yourselves. Don't look out only for your own interests, but take an interest in others, too. PHILIPPIANS 2:3-4

Fix your thoughts on what is true, and honorable, and right, and pure, and lovely, and admirable. Think about things that are excellent and worthy of praise. PHILIPPIANS 4:8

Promises for God's Help

Create in me a clean heart, O God. Renew a loyal spirit within me.
PSALM 51:10

How can you say the LORD does not see your troubles? . . . How can you say God ignores your rights? Have you never heard? Have you never understood? The LORD is the everlasting God, the Creator of all the earth. He never grows weak or weary. No one can measure the depths of his understanding. He gives power to the weak and strength to the powerless.
ISAIAH 40:27-29

Jesus said, "Come to me, all of you who are weary and carry heavy burdens, and I will give you rest." MATTHEW 11:28

I am certain that God, who began the good work within you, will continue his work until it is finally finished on the day when Christ Jesus returns.
PHILIPPIANS 1:6

Don't worry about anything; instead, pray about everything. Tell God what you need, and thank him for all he has done. PHILIPPIANS 4:6

APPENDIX B

RESOURCES FOR FINDING HOPE AND HELP
For more information, check out these resources:

Books

Randy C. Alcorn, *The Purity Principle* (Sisters, Ore.: Multnomah, 2003).

Dan B. Allender, *The Wounded Heart* (Colorado Springs: NavPress, 1995).

Dan B. Allender and Tremper Longman III, *Intimate Allies* (Carol Stream, Ill.: Tyndale, 1995).

Nancy C. Anderson, *Avoiding the Greener Grass Syndrome: How to Grow Affair-Proof Hedges around Your Marriage* (Grand Rapids: Kregel, 2004).

Stephen Arterburn and Fred Stoeker, *Every Man's Battle: Winning the War on Sexual Temptation* (Colorado Springs: WaterBrook, 2000).

Steve Bell and Valerie Bell, *Made to Be Loved: Enjoying Spiritual Intimacy with God and Your Spouse* (Chicago: Moody Press, 1999).

William Cutrer and Sandra Glahn, *Sexual Intimacy in Marriage* (Grand Rapids: Kregel, 1998).

Gregory Godek, *1001 Ways to Be Romantic* (Naperville, Ill.: Casablanca Press, 2000).

John M. Gottman and Joan DeClaire, *The Relationship Cure: A Five-Step Guide to Strengthening Your Marriage, Family, and Friendships* (New York: Three Rivers Press, 2001).

Archibald D. Hart, *The Sexual Man* (Dallas: Word, 1994).

Chip Ingram, *Love, Sex, and Lasting Relationships* (Grand Rapids: Baker, 2003).

Ginger Kolbaba, *Surprised by Remarriage: A Guide to the Happily Even After* (Grand Rapids: Revell, 2006).

Kevin Leman, *Making Sense of the Men in Your Life: What Makes Them Tick, What Ticks You Off, and How to Live in Harmony* (Nashville: Nelson, 2000).

Kevin Leman, *Sheet Music: Uncovering the Secrets of Sexual Intimacy in Marriage* (Carol Stream, Ill.: Tyndale, 2003).

Howard Markman et al., *Fighting for Your Marriage* (San Francisco: Jossey-Bass, 1994).

Louis McBurney and Melissa McBurney, *Real Questions, Real Answers about Sex: The Complete Guide to Intimacy as God Intended* (Grand Rapids: Zondervan, 2005).

Christopher and Rachel McClusky, *When Two Become One: Enhancing Sexual Intimacy in Marriage* (Grand Rapids: Revell, 2004).

Beth Moore, *Breaking Free: Making Liberty in Christ a Reality in Life* (Nashville: B&H, 2000).

Les Parrott and Leslie Parrott, *Saving Your Marriage before It Starts: Seven Questions to Ask before (and after) You Marry* (Grand Rapids: Zondervan, 1995).

Clifford Penner and Joyce Penner, *The Married Guy's Guide to Great Sex: Building a Passionate, Intimate, and Fun Love Life* (Wheaton, Ill.: Tyndale, 2004).

Douglas Rosenau, *A Celebration of Sex* (Nashville: Nelson, 1994).

Eugene Shippen and William Fryer, *The Testosterone Solution: the Hormone that Improves Men's Mental Functions, Sex Drive, and Energy Levels* (New York: M. Evans, 1998).

Gary Smalley, *Connecting with Your Husband* (Carol Stream, Ill.: Tyndale, 2003).

Gary Smalley, *Making Love Last Forever* (Dallas: Word, 1996).

Gary Smalley and Norma Smalley, *For Better or for Best* (Grand Rapids: Zondervan, 1988).

Suzanne Somers, *The Sexy Years: Discover the Hormone Connection* (New York: Crown, 2004).

Steve Stephens, *20 (Surprisingly Simple Rules) and Tools for a Great Marriage* (Carol Stream, Ill.: Tyndale, 2003).

Gary P. Stewart and Timothy J. Demy, *Winning the Marriage Marathon: Six Strategies for Becoming Lifelong Partners* (Grand Rapids: Kregel, 1999).

David Stoop and Jan Stoop, *When Couples Pray Together: Creating Intimacy and Spiritual Wholeness* (Ann Arbor: Vine Books, 2000).

Neil Clark Warren, *Learning to Live with the Love of Your Life* (Wheaton, Ill.: Tyndale, 1995).

Ed Wheat, *Love Life for Every Married Couple: How to Fall in Love, Stay in Love, Rekindle Your Love* (Grand Rapids: Zondervan, 1980).

Ed Wheat and Gaye Wheat, *Intended for Pleasure* (Grand Rapids: Revell, 1997).

Martha Williamson, *Inviting God to Your Wedding* (New York: Harmony Books, 2000).

Magazines

Marriage Partnership, a quarterly magazine published by Christianity Today International; see www.marriagepartnership.com.

NOTES

Chapter 1: It's Not Just about Technique

1. Ephesians 5:31-32.
2. Robert T. Michael et al., *Sex in America: A Definitive Survey* (Boston: Little, Brown, 1994), quoted in Neil Clark Warren, *Learning to Live with the Love of Your Life* (Wheaton, Ill.: Tyndale, 1995), 121.
3. Robert T. Michael, et al., *Sex in America: A Definitive Survey* (Boston: Little, Brown, 1994), quoted in Lisa Collier Cool, "Am I Normal?" *Good Housekeeping* (March 2001): 73.

Chapter 2: Redefining Sex

1. 1 Corinthians 7:3-5.
2. John F. Walvoord and Roy B. Zuck, eds., *The Bible Knowledge Commentary* (Wheaton, Ill.: Victor, 1995), 517.

Chapter 3: What Spouses Need from Each Other

1. Jill Savage, "Scheduling Intimacy?" *Marriage Partnership* (Summer 2005): 21.

Chapter 4: A Wife's Top Three Sex Needs

1. Linda J. Waite and Maggie Gallagher, *The Case for Marriage: Why Married People Are Happier, Healthier, and Better Off Financially* (New York: Doubleday, 2000), 88.
2. Ibid., 96.
3. Clifford Penner and Joyce Penner, *A Married Guy's Guide to Great Sex* (Wheaton, Ill.: Tyndale, 2004), 32.
4. 1 Corinthians 13:5.
5. Gary Smalley and Norma Smalley, *For Better or for Best* (Grand Rapids: Zondervan, 1988), 60.
6. Liberated Christians, "Getting in Touch with Intimacy and Meaningful Sexuality in a Sexually Immature Culture," Liberated Christians, Inc., http://www.libchrist.com/intimacy/intouch.html. Used by permission.
7. Masterpeace Center for Counseling and Development, Online

Resources, "Building the Bridge of a Secure Marriage," http://
www.mpccd.com/resources/resources_buildingbridge.htm.

8. These thoughts are adapted from Neil Clark Warren, *Learning to Live with the Love of Your Life* (Wheaton, Ill.: Tyndale, 1995), 71–75.

9. *UCLA Monthly* (March–April 1981): 1.

10. Gary Smalley and Norma Smalley, *For Better or for Best* (Grand Rapids: Zondervan, 1988), 108.

11. Shirley Glass with Jean Coppock Staeheli, *Not "Just Friends": Protect Your Relationship from Infidelity and Heal the Trauma of Betrayal* (New York: Free Press, 2003), 27.

12. Ibid., 57.

13. Ephesians 5:25.

14. Steve Stephens, *20 Surprisingly Simple Rules and Tools for a Great Marriage* (Carol Stream, Ill.: Tyndale, 2003), 82.

15. Ibid., 82–83.

Chapter 5: A Husband's Top Three Sex Needs

1. Neil Clark Warren, *Learning to Live with the Love of Your Life* (Wheaton, Ill.: Tyndale, 1995), 121.

2. Shaunti Feldhahn, *For Women Only: What You Need to Know about the Inner Lives of Men* (Sisters, Ore.: Multnomah, 2004), 94.

3. David Kantor, quoted in Amy Hertz, "To Love, Honor, and Last Longer than a Year," *O, The Oprah Magazine* (March 2002): 205.

4. John M. Gottman and Joan DeClaire, *The Relationship Cure: A Five-Step Guide to Strengthening Your Marriage, Family, and Friendships* (New York: Three Rivers Press, 2001), 4.

5. Gary Smalley, *Connecting with Your Husband* (Wheaton, Ill.: Tyndale, 2003), 38.

6. Ed Wheat, *Love Life for Every Married Couple* (Grand Rapids: Zondervan, 1997), 78.

7. Kevin Leman, *Sheet Music* (Carol Stream, Ill.: Tyndale, 2003), 46–47, 52.

8. Feldhahn, *For Women Only*, 103.

9. We thank Douglas Rosenau, Debra Taylor, Christopher McCluskey, and Michael Sytsma, excellent Christian sex therapists from Sexual Wholeness Inc., for these insights, which they shared during the

American Marriage and Family Ministries conference, held in Phoenix, Arizona, in 2005.

10. Edward Laumann, Anthony Paik, and Raymond Rosen, "Sexual Dysfunction in the United States: Prevalence and Predictors," *Journal of the American Medical Association* (February 10, 1999).

11. Clifford Penner and Joyce Penner, *The Married Guy's Guide to Great Sex* (Carol Stream, Ill.: Tyndale, 2004), 72.

12. Kevin Leman, *Making Sense of the Men in Your Life* (Nashville: Nelson, 2000), 140.

13. 1 Corinthians 13:4-5.

Chapter 6: A Wife's Other Sex Needs

1. Kelly Maybury, "I Do? Marriage in Uncertain Times," The Gallup Poll, January 22, 2002, http://poll.gallup.com/content/default.aspx?ci=5206.

2. Howard Markman et al., *Fighting for Your Marriage* (San Francisco: Jossey-Bass, 1994), 285, quoted in Gary Smalley, *Making Love Last Forever* (Dallas: Word, 1996), 103.

3. Nick Stinnett and John DeFrain, *Secrets of Strong Families* (Boston: Little, Brown, 1985), quoted in Gary Smalley, *Making Love Last Forever* (Dallas: Word, 1996), 103.

4. Louise Lague, "How Honest Are Couples, Really?" *Reader's Digest*, RD.com, http://www.rd.com/content/openContent.do?contentId=15351.

5. Sue Johnson, quoted in Robert Kiener, "How Honest Are Couples, Really?" *Reader's Digest* (Canada), http://www.readersdigest.ca/mag/2003/04/couples.html.

6. These suggestions were made by Elisa Morgan and Carol Kuykendall, "Spiritual Intimacy," *Marriage Partnership* (Summer 2000): 60.

7. Gregory Godek, *1001 Ways to Be Romantic* (Naperville, Ill.: Casablanca Press, 2000), quoted in *Marriage* (March–April 2002): 10.

8. "Dr. Phil: The Love Survey," *O, The Oprah Magazine* (February 2004): 32.

9. Jim Mueller, "Strategic Romance" growthtrac, Articles, http://www.growthtrac.com/artman/publish/article_15.php.

10. Greg Godek, *1001 Ways to Be Romantic.* Copyright © 1999 by Greg J. P. Godek. Used with permission of Sourcebooks, Inc., 800-432-7444.

Chapter 7: A Husband's Other Sex Needs

1. Kevin Leman, "10 Reasons Your Husband Is Always Thinking about Sex," *Marriage* (March–April 2002): 30.
2. Clifford and Joyce Penner, "You Don't Believe These Sexual Myths, Do You?!" *Marriage* (January–February 1998): 13–15.
3. Paraphrased from Douglas Rosenau, *A Celebration of Sex* (Nashville: Nelson, 1994), 193.
4. David Bjerklie, "When It's Time for Sex, She Knows," *Time* 163, no. 25 (June 21, 2004), http://www.time.com/time/archive/preview/0,10987,994480,00.html.
5. David and Claudia Arp, "Pleasure through All Your Married Years," *Marriage* (November–December 2002): 25.
6. Song of Songs 1:16, 2:3, NIV.

Chapter 8: When Your Libidos Don't Match

1. Gary P. Stewart and Timothy J. Demy, *Winning the Marriage Marathon: Six Strategies for Becoming Lifelong Partners* (Grand Rapids: Kregel, 1999).
2. Archibald Hart, *The Sexual Man* (Nashville: W, 1995), 5.
3. Christopher and Rachel McCluskey, *When Two Become One: Enhancing Sexual Intimacy in Marriage* (Grand Rapids: Revel, 2004), 157–58.
4. Shay Roop, "Nine Reasons Orgasms Are Good for You," *Marriage Partnership* (Summer 2005): 7.
5. Michele Weiner Davis, quoted in "When 'I Do' Becomes 'I Don't Want to'" *USA Today,* January 22, 2003.
6. Lynn Vanderzalm, *Finding Strength in Weakness: Hope and Help for Families Battling Chronic Fatigue Syndrome* (Grand Rapids: Zondervan, 1995), 201.
7. Douglas Rosenau, *A Celebration of Sex* (Nashville: Nelson, 1994), 86.

Chapter 9: When You Are Too Exhausted to Have Sex

1. Susan Crain Bakos, "The Sex Trick Busy Couples Swear By," *Redbook* (March 2001): 125.
2. See 1 Corinthians 7:3-5.
3. David and Claudia Arp, "Partner First, Parent Second," *Marriage* (July–August 2004): 33.

4. See Exodus 20:1-17.

5. Ginger Kolbaba, "Fried!" *Marriage Partnership* (Fall 2005): 52.

Chapter 10: The Elephant in the Bedroom: Talking about Sex

1. Kevin Leman, *Sheet Music* (Carol Stream, Ill.: Tyndale, 2003), 193.

2. "Let's Talk about Sex, Baby," *Marriage Partnership* (Spring 2001): 9.

3. Leman, *Sheet Music*, 193–94.

4. Some of these questions are adapted from our book *40 Unforgettable Dates with your Mate* (Wheaton, Ill.: Tyndale, 2002), 162–64.

5. Leman, *Sheet Music*, 195.

6. Adapted from Louis and Melissa McBurney, "Christian Sex Rules," *Marriage Partnership* (Spring 2001): 34ff; see also http://www.christianitytoday.com/mp/2001/001/4.34.html.

7. 1 Corinthians 6:18-20.

Chapter 11: Keeping the Fun and Excitement in Sex

1. Neil Clark Warren, *Learning to Live with the Love of Your Life* (Wheaton, Ill.: Tyndale, 1995), 123.

Chapter 12: God in the Bedroom

1. PhilipYancey, "Holy Sex: How It Ravishes Our Souls," *Christianity Today* (October 2003): 47.

2. Exodus 6:6-8.

3. Exodus 6:9.

4. Deuteronomy 30:19.

5. Galatians 5:1, NIV.

6. Joel 2:25-27.

7. Zephaniah 3:17.

8. Exodus 6:7.

9. Isaiah 51:12, 15-16, italics added.

10. Isaiah 40:25-29.

11. Philippians 4:6.

12. Lisa Collier Cool, "Am I Normal?" *Good Housekeeping* (March 2001): 74.

13. Kevin Leman, "10 Reasons Your Husband Is Always Thinking about Sex," *Marriage* (March–April 2002): 31.

14. 1 Thessalonians 5:17.

15. Andrew M. Greeley, *Faithful Attraction: Discovering Intimacy, Love, and Fidelity in American Marriage* (New York: Tom Doherty Associates, 1991).

16. Les Parrott and Leslie Parrott, *Saving Your Marriage before It Starts* (Grand Rapids: Zondervan, 1995), 145.

17. Adapted from David Clarke, "Spiritually Alone?" *Marriage Partnership* (Winter 2003): 30.

18. See 1 Peter 3:1-2.

Chapter 13: Facing the Deeper Issues

1. Martha Williamson, *Inviting God to Your Wedding* (New York: Harmony Books, 2000), 84–85.

2. Ibid., 85–86.

3. Hebrews 13:4, NIV.

4. David Goetz, personal conversation.

5. Stephen Arterburn and Fred Stoeker, *Every Man's Battle* (Colorado Springs, Colo.: WaterBrook, 2000), 135–36.

6. Benedict Carey, "The Roots of Temptation," *Los Angeles Times*, October 20, 2003, F1.

7. Elizabeth Enright, "A House Divided," *AARP Magazine* (July–August 2004), http://www.aarpmagazine.org/family/Articles/a2004-05-26-mag-divorce.html.

8. Debbie Layton-Tholl, "Extramarital Affairs: What Is the Allure?" personal Web site, http://hometown.aol.com/affairlady/article.htm.

9. See Matthew 5:31-32.

10. Nancy C. Anderson, *Avoiding the Greener Grass Syndrome* (Grand Rapids: Kregel, 2004), 37.

11. Mary DeMuth, "Opening the Door to Healing," *Marriage Partnership* (Fall 2005): 38.

12. Ibid., 40.

13. Matthew 11:28.

14. Paraphrase of Romans 5:3-5, NIV.

ABOUT THE AUTHORS

DR. GARY AND BARBARA ROSBERG are America's Family Coaches—equipping and encouraging America's families to live and finish life well. Married for more than thirty years, Gary and Barbara have a unique message for couples.

They have committed their ministry to a campaign to Divorce-Proof America's Marriages . . . *for the sake of the next generation.* This campaign equips churches, small groups, and couples to build healthy, biblical marriages.

Together the Rosbergs have written more than a dozen resources, including *The Great Marriage Q & A Book, Six Secrets to a Lasting Love, The Five Love Needs of Men and Women* (2001 Gold Medallion finalist), *Healing the Hurt in Your Marriage, Renewing Your Love: Devotions for Couples, Guard Your Heart* (revised for couples), *40 Unforgettable Dates with Your Mate, Discover the Love of Your Life All Over Again* DVD video series, *Discover the Love of Your Life All Over Again* workbook, *Serving Love* workbook, *Guarding Love* workbook, *Connecting with Your Wife,* and FamilyLife's HomeBuilders Couples Series: *Improving Communication in Your Marriage.*

Gary and Barbara host a nationally syndicated weekday radio program, *America's Family Coaches . . . LIVE!* On this live call-in program, heard in cities all across the country, they coach on many family-related issues. The Rosbergs also host a Saturday radio program that can be heard in the Midwest on the award-winning WHO 1040AM radio.

The Rosbergs have conducted conferences on family and relationship issues in more than one hundred cities across the country. Their flagship conference, *Discover the Love of Your Life All Over Again,* is having an impact on churches and communities nationwide. They have been on the national speaking team for FamilyLife's *Weekend to Remember* conferences since 1988. Gary has also spoken to thousands of men at Promise Keepers stadium events annually since 1996 and to parents and adolescents at Focus on the Family's *Life on the Edge* tour.

GARY, who earned his Ed.D. from Drake University, has been a marriage and family counselor for more than twenty-five years. He founded and coaches CrossTrainers, a weekly Des Moines–area men's ministry comprised of up to five hundred men. Gary serves as the president and member of the board of directors for America's Family Coaches.

BARBARA earned her B.F.A. from Drake University and has authored *Connecting with Your Wife* and co-authored many other books with Gary. She is also a featured speaker for the *Extraordinary Women* video series produced by the American Association of Christian Counselors. Barb serves as executive vice president and member of the board of directors for America's Family Coaches.

The Rosbergs live outside Des Moines, Iowa. They have two married daughters and three grandchildren.

*For more information on the ministries of
America's Family Coaches, contact us at*

AMERICA'S FAMILY COACHES
2540 106th Street, Suite 101
Des Moines, Iowa 50322
1-888-ROSBERG

www.americasfamilycoaches.com

GINGER KOLBABA is the editor of *Marriage Partnership* magazine, a publication of Christianity Today International. She has spoken at national conferences and has appeared on CNN Headline News and Family Life radio. She has also worked as an associate editor for *Today's Christian Woman* and as an assistant editor for *Preaching Today*. Ginger has been a columnist for *Let's Worship* and has published more than one hundred articles. She has authored or coauthored five books, including a Gold Medallion nominee, *Refined by Fire*, and her most recent, *Surprised by Remarriage*. Her first novel, *Secrets from Lulu's Café*, from the Desperate Pastors Wives series, will be released in early 2007. Visit Ginger at www.GingerKolbaba.com.

The Great Marriage Q & A Book

Drawing on real conversations from their nationally syndicated radio call-in show, Gary and Barb Rosberg provide frank and insightful answers to more than 150 frequently asked questions about marriage. From starting off on the right foot, to finishing well, and everything in between, *The Great Marriage Q & A Book* gives you the answers *you* need to make your marriage great.

40 Unforgettable Dates with Your Mate

Bring the zing back into your marriage with *40 Unforgettable Dates with Your Mate*, a book that gives husbands and wives ideas on how they can meet the 5 love needs of their spouse.

6 Secrets to a Lasting Love

Discover the Love of Your Life All Over Again

Everyone wants a marriage that will last a lifetime, and now Gary and Barbara Rosberg have disclosed the 6 secrets that will not only help you create the marriage you've always dreamed of, but one that will last forever. (*Discover the Love of Your Life All Over Again* workbook also available.)

Healing the Hurt in Your Marriage

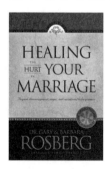

Learn how to forgive past hurts in your marriage, close the loop on unresolved conflict, and restore hope and wholeness in your marriage.

THE 5 SEX NEEDS
OF MEN & WOMEN

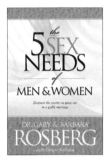

In this follow-up to the best-selling *The 5 Love Needs of Men & Women*, Gary and Barb Rosberg teach couples how to meet each other's most intimate physical, emotional, and spiritual needs and help them develop a godly view of sexual intimacy. Audio read by the authors also available.

THE 5 LOVE NEEDS
OF MEN & WOMEN

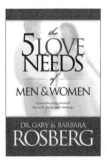

SERVING LOVE

Are you meeting all of your spouse's love needs? Do you even know what they are? Discover the deepest yearnings of your spouse's heart as Gary and Barb Rosberg share the groundbreaking research that shows couples how to meet each other's most intimate needs. (*Serving Love* workbook also available)

GUARD YOUR HEART

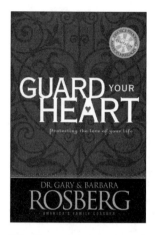

GUARDING LOVE

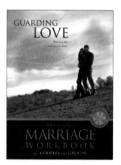

We all need to guard our hearts and marriages. In *Guard Your Heart*, Gary and Barb Rosberg outline the dangers and temptations that can devastate a marriage, and teach couples how to effectively guard their hearts against temptation and strengthen their relationships with each other. (*Guarding Love* workbook also available.)

RENEWING YOUR LOVE

This thirty-day devotional will help couples focus on Scripture, reflect on their marriage, pray together, and set goals that will renew their love.